Lecture Notes of the Institute for Computer Sciences, Social Informatics and Telecommunications Engineering 509

The LNICST series publishes ICST's conferences, symposia and workshops.

LNICST reports state-of-the-art results in areas related to the scope of the Institute. The type of material published includes

- Proceedings (published in time for the respective event)
- Other edited monographs (such as project reports or invited volumes)

LNICST topics span the following areas:

- General Computer Science
- E-Economy
- E-Medicine
- Knowledge Management
- Multimedia
- Operations, Management and Policy
- Social Informatics
- Systems

Jun Zhao
Editor

Wireless and Satellite Systems

13th EAI International Conference, WiSATS 2022
Virtual Event, Singapore, March 12–13, 2023
Proceedings

 Springer

Editor
Jun Zhao (iD)
Nanyang Technological University
Singapore, Singapore

ISSN 1867-8211　　　　　　　　ISSN 1867-822X (electronic)
Lecture Notes of the Institute for Computer Sciences, Social Informatics
and Telecommunications Engineering
ISBN 978-3-031-34850-1　　　　ISBN 978-3-031-34851-8 (eBook)
https://doi.org/10.1007/978-3-031-34851-8

This Springer imprint is published by the registered company Springer Nature Switzerland AG
The registered company address is: Gewerbestrasse 11, 6330 Cham, Switzerland

Preface

We are delighted to introduce the proceedings of the fourteenth edition of the European Alliance for Innovation (EAI) International Conference on Wireless and Satellite Systems (WiSATS 2022). The conference brought together researchers, developers, and practitioners from around the world who are utilizing and advancing wireless communication technologies, as well as satellite and space communication technologies. The conference's central theme was the means of providing wireless and satellite services directly to the user for personal communications, multimedia and location identification.

The technical program of WiSATS 2022 consisted of 9 full papers. The conference tracks included early track, main track, invited track, and last-minute track. The presentations allowed for technical discussions of the research methodologies, techniques, and findings that underpin the development of advanced technologies for improving the security, privacy, efficiency, and reliability of wireless communication and satellite systems. Aside from the high-quality technical paper presentations, the technical program also featured three keynote speeches. The three keynote speakers were Peng Li from University of Aizu, Japan, Qing Yang from University of North Texas, USA and Pengyuan Zhou from University of Science and Technology of China. Through these technical presentations and keynote speeches, attendees gained insights into the latest advancements in the field and discussed potential collaborations for future research and development.

Coordination with the steering chair Imrich Chlamtac and general chair Tony Q.S. Quek was essential for the success of the conference. We would like to extend our sincere appreciation for their unwavering support and guidance provided to us. It was a great honor to collaborate with an exceptional organizing committee team, whose diligent efforts in organizing and supporting the conference were invaluable to its success. In particular, the Technical Program Committee, led by our TPC Chair and Co-chair: Jun Zhao (Nanyang Technological University, Singapore) and Abbas Jamalipour (University of Sydney, Australia) completed the peer-review process of technical papers and made a high-quality technical program. We are also grateful to all the authors who submitted their papers to WiSATS 2022.

We hold a firm conviction that the WiSATS 2022 conference offered a comprehensive platform for researchers, developers, and practitioners to engage in discussions on all relevant science and technology aspects related to wireless communication and satellite systems. Based on the contributions presented in this volume, we anticipate that future WiSATS conferences will be equally successful and thought-provoking.

May 2023   Jun Zhao

Organization

Steering Committee

Imrich Chlamtac   University of Trento, Italy

Organizing Committee

General Chair

Tony Q. S. Quek   Singapore University of Technology and Design, Singapore

TPC Chair and Co-chair

Jun Zhao   Nanyang Technological University, Singapore
Abbas Jamalipour   University of Sydney, Australia

Sponsorship and Exhibit Chair

Lingyang Song   Peking University, China

Local Chair

Yichao Feng   Nanyang Technological University, Singapore

Workshops Chairs

Gang Wang   Beihang University, China
Huimei Han   Zhejiang University of Technology, China
Jie Feng   Nanyang Technological University, Singapore

Publicity and Social Media Chair

Yong Zeng   Southeast University, China

Publications Chair

Osman Yagan   Carnegie Mellon University, USA

Web Chair

Sudhan Majhi   Indian Institute of Science Bangalore, India

Technical Program Committee

Xuebin Ren	Xi'an Jiaotong University, China
Huimei Han	Zhejiang University of Technology, China
Lei Yang	University of Nevada, Reno, USA
Xiaowen Gong	Auburn University, USA
Xu Chen	Sun Yat-sen University, China
Xinyu Zhou	Nanyang Technological University, Singapore
Chang Liu	Nanyang Technological University, Singapore
Zelei Cheng	Purdue University, USA
Mingzhe Chen	Princeton University, USA
Sudhan Majhi	Indian Institute of Science Bangalore, India
Yong Zeng	Southeast University, China
Gang Wang	Beihang University, China
Lingyang Song	Peking University, China
Ziyao Liu	Nanyang Technological University, Singapore
Jiale Guo	Nanyang Technological University, Singapore

Contents

Network Efficiency and Reliability

Security and Privacy in Healthcare, Transportation, and Satellite Networks

TF-Net: Deep Learning Empowered Tiny Feature Network for Night-Time UAV Detection

Maham Misbah[1], Misha Urooj Khan[1], Zhaohui Yang[2], and Zeeshan Kaleem[1(✉)]

[1] Department of Electrical and Computer Engineering, COMSATS University Islamabad, Wah Campus, Wah Cantt., Pakistan
`zeeshankaleem@gmail.com`
[2] College of Information Science and Electronic Engineering, Zhejiang University, Hangzhou 310027, China
`yang_zhaohui@zju.edu.cn`

Abstract. Technological advancements have normalized the usage of unmanned aerial vehicles (UAVs) in every sector, spanning from military to commercial but they also pose serious security concerns due to their enhanced functionalities and easy access to private and highly secured areas. Several instances related to UAVs have raised security concerns, leading to UAV detection research studies. Visual techniques are widely adopted for UAV detection, but they perform poorly at night, in complex backgrounds, and in adverse weather conditions. Therefore, a robust night vision-based drone detection system is required to that could efficiently tackle this problem. Infrared cameras are increasingly used for nighttime surveillance due to their wide applications in night vision equipment. This paper uses a deep learning-based TinyFeatureNet (TF-Net), which is an improved version of YOLOv5s, to accurately detect UAVs during the night using infrared (IR) images. In the proposed TF-Net, we introduce architectural changes in the neck and backbone of the YOLOv5s. We also simulated four different YOLOv5 models (s,m,n,l) and proposed TF-Net for a fair comparison. The results showed better performance for the proposed TF-Net in terms of precision, IoU, GFLOPS, model size, and FPS compared to the YOLOv5s. TF-Net yielded the best results with 95.7% precision, 84% mAp, and 44.8% *IoU*.

Keywords: YOLOv5s · TinyFeatureNet · Night Vision · UAVs · Challenging environmental conditions · Drone Detection

1 Introduction

Unmanned aerial vehicles (UAVs) are increasingly becoming popular owing to the technological advancements and increased use cases [26]. Initially, drones

This work was supported by the Higher Education Commission (HEC), Pakistan under the NRPU 2021 Grant 15687.

were only used for military purposes, but now they are used in many other fields [19]. Currently, the commercial and military industries that rely on UAVs are expanding rapidly, attracting investors who are driving improvements in UAV technology and continuously trying to reduce the size, weight, and prices. Drones started off with bigger size, but as technology advanced, they became smaller and more intelligent [11]. Consequently, these smaller drones have prompted security concerns as they can easily reach any private area [4,5,11].

A lot of research has been conducted to date for the detection of UAVs using visual [7,8,10], radio frequency (RF) [22], acoustic [11], thermal [24] and radar methods [6]. But many of them show poor performance during night and in extreme weather conditions. Therefore it is crucial to have a night vision-based drone detection system [25]. The use of infrared cameras for nighttime monitoring has become quite common [4,6,24] due to the use of night vision technology in surveillance and protection [9,12]. The military, law enforcement, and the general public, all sectors have applications where it could be deployed and used effectively. The difficult challenge of overcoming UAV detection at night time could be overcome by the use high-priced and high resolution thermal imaging devices. These high-priced devices have also some limitations like inefficiency in low-light conditions, such as complete darkness, or poor atmospheric conditions when the captured image does not accurately reflect the true things being seen [19].

The worldwide terrorism problem has expanded this domain into the areas of individual safety, border control, national security, and military surveillance [31]. That's why the development of IR based object detection and classification are among the fastest topics being worked on [4,6,24]. Currently, convolutional neural networks (CNNs) are the most effective models for detecting objects [3,30]. AlexNet's groundbreaking performance in the *2012 ImageNet Large Scale Visual Recognition Challenge* [14] marked a turning point for the image recognition challenge. When applied to the RGB domain, CNNs greatly improved the efficiency of object identification. Girshick et al. [30] introduced labeled Regions with CNN (R-CNN) whose training process is quite time-consuming. Fast R-CNN [8] was presented to deal with issues that could not be solved by R-CNN. Faster R-CNN [21], developed by Shaoqing Ren et al., is an object identification system that removed the selective search strategy and allowed the network to learn region proposals. In contrast to region-based algorithms, You Only Look Once (YOLO) is an approach to object detection [20]. It works similarly to DNN-based regression [29], predicting the existence of an item and its bounding box for a fixed-size grid that tiles the input picture. It requires a single run through the network for detection.

The use of such frameworks for IR images is hindered by the scarcity of large data sets and the expensive cost of an IR camera. We thoroughly searched the literature but saw only a few number of studies that addressed the drone detection at night utilizing IR images with extreme weather conditions. IR-based UAV data sets captured in outdoor settings with poor atmospheric quality, particularly at night, was also lacking. In this paper, we perform multi-model UAV detection based on IR images captured at night using YOLOv5 and proposed

Tiny Feature Network (TF-Net) in complex backgrounds. The main contributions of this paper are listed below:

- To efficiently detect UAVs during the night, we employ UAV detection based on IR images. Relatively less work has been done on IR-based object detection in the literature. To the best of our knowledge, this is the first study considering IR-based UAV detection using proposed TF-Net, YOLOv5s, YOLOv5m, YOLOv5l and YOLOv5n.
- In complex backgrounds, it becomes quite challenging to detect any type and size of UAV. We address this problem by making a dataset that consisted IR based UAV images with multiple complex environmental background and weather conditions.
- For performance enhancement, we proposed TF-Net, an improved version of YOLOv5s by the introduction kernel based modifications in the neck and backbone.
- For a fair comparison, we trained all considered models with same dataset, learning rate, warmup setup and epochs with early stopping.
- The proposed TF-Net detects multi-size and muti-type UAVs with increased precision. Using TF-Net improves the results in terms of precision, mAp@0.5, IoU, model size, and, GFLOPs compared to the baseline YOLOv5 models.

2 Literature Review

UAVs have grown in popularity for a wide range of uses. Many incidents involving the illegal use of UAVs is making it quite difficult to regulate them and mitigate the associated privacy risks. Real-time drone identification is urgently needed to shield high-security places from the risk of drone intrusion. Currently, there are two major challenges to drone identification in real time. One of them is the rapid speed with which drones move, which calls for equally rapid detection systems. Secondly, multiple sizes of drones further complicate the detection process. A novel approach for detecting multi-rotor drones was presented in [15]. They replaced the YOLOv5s backbone with Efficientlite, which allowed them to streamline the model by eliminating unnecessary parameters. To compensate for the accuracy loss, adaptive spatial feature fusion was introduced in the head block to enable the fusion of feature maps with varying spatial resolutions. To speed up network convergence, an angle limitation was added to the existing regression loss function. They trained and validated the model using a dataset of 1,259 multi-rotor UAV images. The modified Yolov5s displayed enhanced detection performance in terms of precision, recall, and mAp, at 92.32%, 89.52%, and 91.76% respectively. [16], evaluated RetinaNet, fully convolutional one-stage object detector (FCOS), YOLOv3, and YOLOv4. They reduced the size of YOLOv4's convolutional channels and shortcut layer and improved the accuracy of small drone detection. 10,000 drone images were captured with Oneplus phone camera. Results showed that the improved-YOLOv4 model achieved 90.5% mAP. Authors in [17] taried, CNN, support vector machine (SVM), and k-nearest neighbor (KNN) to train a drone-bird dataset and achieved a maximum accuracy of 93%.

For detecting low-altitude UAVs, authors in [27] found that YOLOv4 was more effective than YOLOv3 in terms of both accuracy and speed. Due to lack of publicly available low-altitude dataset, they created their own by using three drone models-the DJI-Phantom, Inspire, and XIRO-Xplorer and combined their data with online drone images. They trained the YOLO models with a batch size of 64, 0.9 momentum, 0.0005 decay and 100,000. YOLOv4 achieved 89.32% accuracy which was 5.18% better than YOLOv3. To address the security problems posed by UAVs, [23] differentiated two kinds of drones and separated them from birds. They trained their model using a dataset of 10,000 visual images having many drone types like multi rotors, helicopters, and birds. The trained model achieved an accuracy and mAp of 83% and 84%, respectively. Schumann et al. [24] used median-background subtraction in conjunction with a deep learning-based region proposal network (RPN) and VGG-conv5 as a classifier. Their dataset had 10,286 images and won first place in the 2017 drone vs. bird competition. In [25], background-subtraction method was used for the identification of the moving items. They classified the detected items into three categories: bird, drone, and background using MobileNet-v2. This method produced encouraging results with accuracy, recall, and f-score of 70.1%, 78.8%, and 74.2% respectively.

An anti-drone system with automatic identification for the attacking drones was presented by Khan et al. [13]. Radar which emitted microwaves is used to find moving objects and then YOLOv3 was used to identify the category of object identified by the activated the camera. If the identification confidence was more than 75%, then the laser gun was used to lock the identified object. Study in [3] fine-tuned YOLOv5 model on a publicly accessible dataset of 1359 images. They dataset was also augmented to overcome the missing data points. They compared to results with baseline standard YOLOv3, YOLOv4, and maskRCNN. The suggested technique was more effective with 95.2% accuracy. The work in [6] used Darknet as the YOLOv4 backbone for UAV and bird detection. The proposed approach successfully overcame the major difficulty of identifying comparable tiny objects near and distant in all situations, with 98.3% detection accuracy.

Images captured by thermal cameras are unaffected by smoke or other atmospheric factors, making them an indispensable tool for use in search-and-rescue operations and fire prevention. In [18], a Faster RCNN was used to examine thermal and visual spectrum images side by side. For object recognition and classification at the sea's surface, authors in [22] studied UAV thermal pictures for easy identification and location of aquatic objects. The experimental findings revealed a 92.5% accuracy across a testing dataset. The study in [28] presented a multi-sensor fully autonomous drone detection system with a thermal infrared camera. The proposed system reduced the false positives by employing sensor fusion to make it more reliable than individual systems. To tackle the unavailability of the datasets in this domain, this paper also presented annotated video datasets with 650 visible and IR videos of birds, airplanes, helicopters, and drones [32].

3   Proposed TinyFeatureNet (TF-Net)

The proposed TF-Net has four blocks: input, backbone, neck, and head. To facilitate speedy inference with no mAP cost, the *input block* maps spatial information from the input imagery to the channel dimension. It also performs data preparation by using mosaic data augmentation (MDA) and adaptive image filling (AIF) techniques. Training time and the need for a tiny mini-batch size is reduced due to MDA's ability to teach the TF-Net object identification on a lesser scale than conventional object detection methods. The cross-stage partial network (CSP) and spatial pyramid pooling (SPP) are used by the *backbone block* to extract feature maps of varying sizes from the input pictures. The calculation and inference times were further reduced by using the BottleneckCSP block. For precise detection, SPP helped by the extraction of feature maps at three different scales. Feature pyramid network (FPN) is used in *neck block*, which captures semantic attributes from the highest to lowest levels of the hierarchy. The final detection is provided by the last *head block*. Anchor boxes are sets of bounding boxes that have been labeled in terms of their height and width. In order to record the scale and aspect ratio of different object classes, these boxes are selected depending on the item sizes in training datasets. In TF-Net, we used 8×8 (P3), 16×16 (P4) and 32×32 (P5) anchor boxes for the identification of target objects. Overall TF-Net uses a single neural network to analyze the whole image. It partitions the input image of $416 \times 416 \times 3$ into grids and provides probabilistic bounding box predictions for each grid cell. The projected probability then weights the bounding boxes with precise predictions after only one forward propagation through the neural network. Then the max suppression strategy guarantees that the TF-Net only performs one identification for each item. The size of the kernels used for the head and backbone impacts the extracted features, training parameters, gradients, and GFLOPs. The detailed TF-Net model network structure is shown in Fig 1. Proposed TF-Net determined the best kernel size for feature maps which excellently performed UAV detection during night time in bad weather conditions. The model depth multiple and layer channel multiples are 0.33 and 0.50, respectively.

TF-Net uses cross-entropy function for a cost function. To prevent the model from over-fitting, we added mixed regularization $L1$ and $L2$ to the loss function. Adding mixed regularization makes the model more robust for night time detection. Loss function L is optimized as follows:

$$
\begin{aligned}
C\_L &= G(a, b) = -\sum_i a(i) \ln b(i) \\
L &= C\_L + \sum_j \left(\alpha \, |\psi_j| + (1 - \alpha)\psi_j^2 \right),
\end{aligned}
\tag{1}
$$

where a and b represent the actual and predicted probability distribution of x, respectively, α represents the regularization parameter and ψ represents weights. Before computing $L1$ and $L2$ mixed regularization, the average cross-entropy of the whole batch is computed to avoid over-fitting.

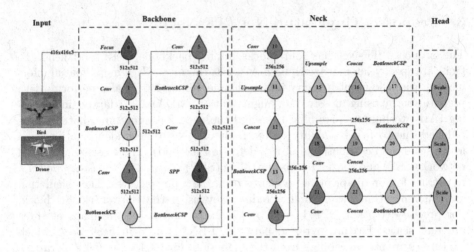

Fig. 1. Proposed **TF-Net Model**.

4 Dataset and Implementation

The detection of drones is quite difficult at night because it gets harder to see them with nake eye. In this study, we assessed the performance of TF-Net and YOLOv5s,m,l and n for nighttime UAV detection. We consider a dataset with more than 3000 images of UAVs flying at night in various backgrounds [2]. We set the train-test ratio to 8:2 with 3100 training and 791 test images. Dataset visualization shown in Fig. 2a depicts the multi-size UAVs target. YOLO based object detection models need datasets with class categories, bounding boxes, and annotation files. We used *Roboflow* [1], an open-source dataset platform, to create a dataset that had all the necessary files for the TF-Net and YOLOv5 models. Initially, the images are pre-processed, by resizing them all to a fixed dimension size of 416 × 416 scaling, contrast enhancement before training. We configure the hyper-parameters as described in Table. 1 to have smooth data training without higher loss and over-fitting. Adam's and the SGD optimizer's initial learning rate (lr0) was set to 0.1. The one-cycle learning rate (lrf) was changed to be 0.1. The momentum for the SGD optimizer was set at 0.937 with a weight decay of 0.0005. At the warmup epoch of 3.0, the initial warmup momentum is 0.8 and the initial warmup bias is 0.1. Box loss gain, class loss gain, object loss gain, and focused loss gamma all have initial values of zero. The multiple threshold is 4.0, and the *IoU* training threshold is 0.20. All models are trained on Google Colab with a K80 GPU and 12 GB RAM. During training,

Table 1. Hyper-parameters qualitative analysis.

Input size	Epochs	Layers	Learning rate	Momentum	Weight Decay
416× 416	300	232	0.01	0.937	0.0005

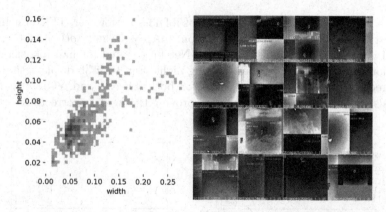

Fig. 2. Data Set (a) Distribution (b) Ground-truth images.

the objectness loss decreased from 0.019 to 0.014 and the box loss decreased from 0.09 to 0.04. The classifier head is trained to identify the type of the target item using a classification loss. Values range from 0.035 to 0.010. An enhanced classification loss has been seen for the suggested approach. The precision, recall, mAp, and IoU over 100 plus epochs show an increasing trend, which implies that the model's learning patterns are going well. These results still have room for improvement, which will be addressed in the future work.

5 Results and Discussions

YOLOv5l has a depth multiple (DM) of 1.0 and a width multiple (WM) of 1.0. YOLOv5m shows 0.67 DM and 0.75 WM, YOLOv5s and TF-Net has 0.33 DM with a WM of 0.50 while YOLOv5n has 0.33 DM with a WM of 0.25. YOLOv5l is the deepest model and takes the largest to train due to its increased convolution and computational complexity while YOLOv5n takes the least and has the lowest computational complexity but the evaluation metrics computed for both these are lower as compared to YOLOv5s and TF-Net. We assess the performance of the proposed TF-Net and YOLOv5 (s,ml and n) by calculating true positive (TP), true negative (TN), false positive (FP), and false negative (FN), precision (P), recall (R), mean accuracy precision (mAp), and intersection over union (IoU).

5.1 Performance Evaluation

YOLOV5n, YOLOv5s, YOLOv5m, and YOLOv5l achieved a precision of 92.3%, 93.1%, 91.2%, and 90.8%, respectively. YOLOv5l had the lowest precision among all the models which shows its decreased sensitivity for UAV detection in night. In terms of recall, YOLOv5m performed well by achieving 78.1% compared to the rest of the YOLOv5 models and TF-Net. The highest precision of 93.1% is achieved by YOLOv5s. Similarly, YOLOv5m has the highest mAp@0.5 of

83.3% while YOLOv5n has the highest IoU of 43.5%. However, TF-Net achieved the best of all when it comes to precision, mAp@0.5, and IoU of 95.6%, 84% and 44.8% respectively. This makes TF-Net best suited for multiple-size UAV detection in complex backgrounds during night. Fig. 3a & 3b displays the recall and precision results over 180 epochs for both TF-Net and YOLOv5. These graphs show an increasing trend, hence proving the model's correctness.

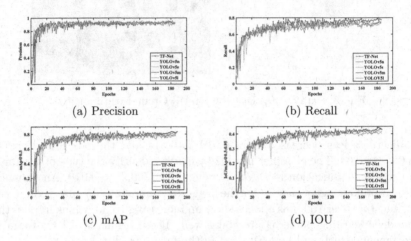

(a) Precision

(b) Recall

(c) mAP

(d) IOU

Fig. 3. Graphical representation of the merged dataset.

The proposed TF-Net outperforms all the YOLOv5 models (s,m,l,n) in terms of precision, mAp@0.5, and IoU as shown in Table 2. TF-Net achieved 95.7% precision which is 3.4% higher than YOLOv5n, 2.1% higher than YOLOv5s, 4.5% higher than YOLOv5m and 4.9% higher than YOLOv5l. YOLOv5s achieved 1% higher recall than TF-Net. Compared to other YOLOv5 models, TF-Net achieved 77% recall which is 1.4% higher than YOLOv5n, 0.7% higher than YOLOv5m and 2.1% higher than YOLOv5l. TF-Net's, mAp@0.5, and IoU are also higher by 84% and 44.8%, respectively. This shows the higher sensitivity of TF-Net for detecting multi-size objects compared to the rest of the standard YOLOv5 models during night time.

After training over 200 epochs, TF-Net has the highest true positive (TP) rate of 82 which is 2% higher than YOLOv5n, 1% higher than YOLOv5s and 5% higher than YOLOv5l. YOLOv5s yielded slightly less TP rate of 81%. YOLOv5s has the same number of network layers as TF-Net but the kernel and feature-map sizes are different. TP rate is also referred to as "Sensitivity". This shows that the TF-Net model is most sensitive to multi-size UAV detection and will have excellent sensitivity upon recalling and correctly identifying drones as drones.

Table 2. Training Evaluation Metrics.

Model	TP	FN	Precision (%)	Recall (%)	mAp @0.5 (%)	IoU (%)
TF-Net	82	18	**95.7**	77.4	**84**	**44.8**
YOLOv5n	80 (↓ 2)	20 (↑ 2)	92.3 (↓ 3.4)	76 (↓ 1.4)	80.5 (↓ 3.5)	43.5 (↓ 1.3)
YOLOv5s	81 (↓ 1)	19 (↑ 1)	93.1 (↓ 2.6)	**78.4 (↑ 1)**	80.3 (↓ 3.7)	43.4 (↓ 1.4)
YOLOv5m	**83 (↑ 1)**	**17 (↓ 1)**	91.2 (↓ 4.5)	78.1(↑ 0.7)	83.6 (↓ 0.4)	43.3 (↓ 1.5)
YOLOv5l	77 (↓ 5)	23 (↑ 5)	90.8 (↓ 4.9)	75.3 (↓ 2.1)	82.9 (↓ 1.1)	42.2 (↓ 2.6)

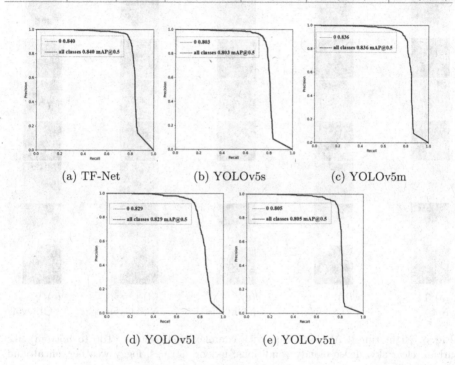

(a) TF-Net   (b) YOLOv5s   (c) YOLOv5m

(d) YOLOv5l   (e) YOLOv5n

Fig. 4. Precision-Recall Curve.

The plot in Fig. 3c & 3d shows mAp@0.5 and *IoU* of all trained models, respectively. mAp@0.5 and *IoU* of the TF-Net have significantly improved compared to the YOLOv5 models. The mAP value compares the ground-truth bounding box to the detected box and returns a score. The higher mAP score of TFNet shows its ability for accurate detection. TF-Net mAp increased by 3.5% w.r.t YOLOv5n, 3.7% w.r.t YOLOv5s, 0.4% w.r.t YOLOv5m and 1.1% w.r.t YOLOv5. The *IoU* of TF-Net increased by 1.3% w.r.t YOLOv5n, 1.4% w.r.t YOLOv5s, 1.5% w.r.t YOLOv5m and 2.6% w.r.t YOLOv5. Although there is always a trade-off between mAp and *IoU* but in our case, both metrics have shown improvement which specifies that TF-Net excellent ability to overlap between the predicted and ground truth bounding box. The precision-recall curves shown in Fig. 4 give the value of mAp@0.5. The precision-recall curve in Fig. 4a achieved the highest mAp@0.5 of 84% for TF-Net. Comparatively, lower mAp@0.5 is achieved by YOLOv5s, YOLOv5m, YOLOv5l, and YOLOv5n.

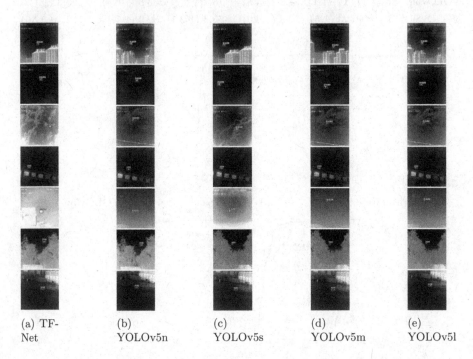

| (a) TF-Net | (b) YOLOv5n | (c) YOLOv5s | (d) YOLOv5m | (e) YOLOv5l |

Fig. 5. Night time UAV Detection with complex backgrounds (Top to bottom) like urban, clear sky, dense cloudy conditions, indoor settings, foggy weather, shrub and low altitude.

5.2   Model Performance Under Varying Environmental Backgrounds and Conditions

To understand the impact of varying environmental backgrounds on detection performance, we compare the results of the proposed TF-Net with YOLOv5 models w.r.t different backgrounds including clearsky, urban, dense cloudy, indoor settings, foggy, shrub, and at low altitude in Fig. 5. TF-Net achieved 93% accuracy in the urban background compared to the YOLOv5s (89% accuracy).

Similarly, for dense cloudy and indoor settings, TF-Net performed well with 88% and 91% accuracy, respectively. For foggy background, TF-Net yielded 4% better accuracy than YOLOv5 models. TF-Net also performed better by achieving 13% and 3% higher accuracy in the case of shrubs and low-altitude UAVs, respectively. But TF-Net yielded better results in detecting UAVs at high altitudes compared to low altitudes. YOLOv5m achieves a detection accuracy of 87% in urban, 88% in a clear sky, and 83% in dense cloudy conditions, which is comparatively less than the TF-Net. Similarly, YOLOv5l achieved 9%, 10%, and 5% less detection accuracy compared to TF-Net in an urban, clear sky and dense cloudy situation, respectively. The worst performance is shown by YOLOv5n with a detection accuracy of 77% in dense cloudy conditions, 70% in indoor, and 75% in foggy weather. For low-altitude UAV detection, YOLOv5m remained the least sensitive with a detection accuracy of 79%. Here, TF-Net is proved to be a better choice for UAV detection in all backgrounds and altitudes.

5.3   Model Performance for Multi-size Target

The modified kernel size enables the proposed TF-Net network to perform well on multi-size images. Figure 6 shows multi-size UAV detection by TF-Net. Despite being lightweight, TF-Net efficiently detected small, medium, and large UAVs with a detection accuracy of 90%, 91%, and 91%, respectively. YOLOv5s achieved 3%, 4%, and 2% less detection accuracy on small, medium and, large UAVs, respectively compared to TF-Net. Among all four YOLOv5 models, YOLOv5s achieved higher accuracy's for multiple scale targets. The worst detection accuracy of 77% is shown by YOLOv5l on medium sized drones. Highest accuracy's are shown by TF-Net on multiple sized UAV targets. This indicates the effectiveness and sensitivity of the proposed TF-Net model to detect UAVs of any target size in complex backgrounds.

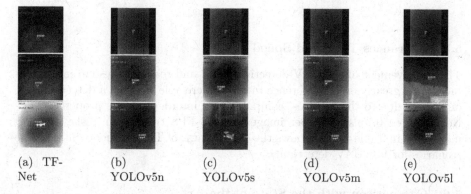

(a) TF-   (b)   (c)   (d)   (e)
Net   YOLOv5n   YOLOv5s   YOLOv5m   YOLOv5l

Fig. 6. Detection results of Multi-size IR AV targets (Top to bottom) small, medium and large.

5.4   Models Computational Complexity

The system's computational complexity depends on training epochs plus time, trained model size with layers, and GFLOPs. For real-time object detection, it is important to have a lightweight model. In our case, the model size decreased to 10.8 MB, making it suitable and efficient for real-time UAV detection. For YOLOv5s, YOLOv5m, and YOLOv5l, the model size was 14.8 MB, 42.1 MB, and 92.8 MB. This depicts a 4% decrease in TF-Net model size compared to the YOLOv5s. TF-Net was trained for 292 epochs using 232 layers and extracted 5222070 parameters with 75.2 GFLOPs. TF-Net has higher GFLOPs compared to YOLOv5s (16.7 GFLOPs) despite having the same number of network layers. The remaining training parameters are listed in Table 4. The concept of early stopping was employed here and 300 epochs were given as input epoch to all models. Table 3 shows that each models stopped at different epoch. YOLOv5l stopped at the earliest epoch of 186 and has the highest GFLOPs of 107.6 while TF-Net stopped at 292 epoch. YOLOv5n took the least training time of 1.2 h with a trained model size of 3.8 MB. Thus, TF-Net has the most comparable computational complexity with good GFLOPs performance (75.2), low trained model size (10.8 MB) plus layers (232) and high precision (95.7%).

Table 3. Computational Complexity.

Model	Epochs	Training Time (Hrs)	Size (MB)	Layers	GFLOPs
TF-Net	**292**	**4.5**	**10.8**	**232**	**75.2**
YOLOv5n	200 (↓ 92)	1.2 (↓ 3.3)	3.8 (↓ 7)	213 (↓ 19)	4.1 (↓71.1)
YOLOv5s	230 (↓ 62)	1.6(↓ 2.9)	14.8 (↑ 4)	232 (same)	16.7 (↓ 58.5)
YOLOv5m	202 (↓ 90)	2.4 (↓ 2.1)	42.1 (↑ 31.3)	290 (↑58)	47.9 (↓ 27.3)
YOLOv5l	186 (↓ 106)	3.1 (↓ 1.4)	92.8 (↑ 82)	367 (↑135)	107.6 (↑ 32.4)

5.5   Inferences Time and Speed

The improvement of the UAV detection speed and real-time system implementation rely greatly on the inference rate. We were able to reach a detection time of 10.2 ms due to the features' computational interdependence properties. TF-Net achieved 0.7 ms NMS per image with 98 FPS trained on Tesla T4 GPU mentioned in Table 4. This shows the effectiveness of TF-Net model in real time scenarios for fast UAV detection.

5.6   Comparison with the State-of-the-Art

We compare our results with the state-of-the-art models for UAV detection based on YOLOv4 and YOLOv5 models. It is apparent from Table 5 that TF-Net performed well in terms of precision, FPS, and model size compared to the

Table 4. Model Evaluation on Test Data.

Model	Pre-process (ms)	Inference(ms)	NMS per image (ms)	FPS
TF-Net	**0.3**	**10.2**	**0.7**	**98**
YOLOv5n	0.3 (same)	8.4 ($\downarrow$ 1.8)	0.9 ($\uparrow$ 0.2)	119 ($\uparrow$ 21)
YOLOv5s	0.3(same)	9.3 ($\uparrow$ 0.2)	0.7(same)	107 ($\uparrow$ 9)
YOLOv5m	0.4 ($\uparrow$ 0.1)	14 ($\uparrow$ 3.8)	0.9 ($\uparrow$ 0.2)	71 ($\downarrow$ 27)
YOLOv5l	0.3(same)	15.4 ($\uparrow$ 5.2)	0.7(same)	64 ($\downarrow$ 34)

Table 5. Comparison With the State-of-the-Art.

Model	Dataset (images)	Input size	Precision (%)	FPS	Parameters (Millions)	CPU/GPU
TF-Net	**3891**	416×416	**95.7**	**98**	**5.2**	**NVIDIA Tesla T4**
Improved YOLOv5 [15]	1259	640×640	94.96	N/G	7.02	NVIDIA GeForce RTX 3050
Pruned YOLOv4 [16]	10,000	416×416	74.2	43	63.9	Tesla P100
Real-time Drone Detection Algorithm [25]	24,075	N/G	70.1	9.5	N/G	NVIDIA GeForce GT 1030
YOLOv4 [27]	4032	416×416	89.32	38	N/G	N/G
YOLOv5 [3]	1359	416×416	94.7	N/G	87	NVidia RTX2070

other literature models. TF-Net outperformed all other models and achieved 95.7% precision. When compared to [8,22] and [29], TF-Net has the highest FPS of 98. TF-Net also proved to be light-weight with a trained model size of 10 MB and 5.2 million parameters as compared to [4]. Therefore we implemented night vision UAV detection utilizing the proposed TF-Net model with IR images and achieved superior results compared to the literature and baseline models.

6   Conclusion

We proposed an improved version of the YOLOv55s based object detection model TF-Net to improve UAV detection in adverse weather conditions at night, where each input image was adaptively enhanced to obtain better detection performance. Kernel-based feature-map extraction was used to extract weather-specific target information for the TF-Net detector, whose hyper-parameters are set to attain excellently optimized results. Moreover, the whole framework was trained in an end-to-end fashion, where the parameter prediction network was weakly supervised to learn small sized feature maps with less detection loss. By taking advantage of excellent training, early screening, and feature map based prediction, our proposed approach was able to adaptively handle normal and adverse weather conditions. The experimental results showed that our method performed much better than previous approaches in both the foggy and low-light scenarios. The proposed TF-Net model performed well in terms of precision, model size, mAp@0.5, IoU and GFLOPs compared to the baseline YOLOv5 models. The TF-Net achieved 4.5% higher precision, compared to the baseline YOLOv5 model.

References

1. Give your software the power to see objects in images and video. https://roboflow.com/. Accessed 18 Nov 2022
2. UAV_IR computer vision project. https://universe.roboflow.com/uav-project-eia1l/uav_ir. Accessed 18 Nov 2022
3. Al-Qubaydhi, N., et al.: Detection of unauthorized unmanned aerial vehicles using YOLOv5 and transfer learning. Electronics **11**(17), 2669 (2022). https://doi.org/10.3390/electronics11172669
4. Anwar, M.Z., Kaleem, Z., Jamalipour, A.: Machine learning inspired sound-based amateur drone detection for public safety applications. IEEE Trans. Veh. Technol. **68**(3), 2526–2534 (2019). https://doi.org/10.1109/tvt.2019.2893615
5. Chen, M., Yang, Z., Saad, W., Yin, C., Poor, H.V., Cui, S.: A joint learning and communications framework for federated learning over wireless networks. IEEE Trans. Wirel. Commun. **20**(1), 269–283 (2020)
6. Dadrass Javan, F., Samadzadegan, F., Gholamshahi, M., Ashatari Mahini, F.: A modified YOLOv4 deep learning network for vision-based UAV recognition. Drones **6**(7), 160 (2022). https://doi.org/10.3390/drones6070160
7. Dil, M., et al.: SafeSpace MFNet: precise and efficient multifeature drone detection network. arXiv preprint arXiv:2211.16785, pp. 1–13 (2022)
8. Girshick, R.: Fast R-CNN. In: 2015 IEEE International Conference on Computer Vision (ICCV) (2015). https://doi.org/10.1109/iccv.2015.169
9. Jamalipour, A., Kaleem, Z., Lorenz, P., Choi, W.: Special issue on amateur drone and UAV communications and networks. J. Commun. Netw. **20**(5), 429–433 (2018)
10. Kaleem, Z., Khan, M.U., Dil, M., Misbah, M., Orakzai, F.A., Alam, M.Z.: Deep learning empowered fast and accurate multiclass UAV detection in challenging weather conditions. preprints202212.0049.v1 (2022)
11. Kaleem, Z., Rehmani, M.H.: Amateur drone monitoring: state-of-the-art architectures, key enabling technologies, and future research directions. IEEE Wirel. Commun. **25**(2), 150–159 (2018). https://doi.org/10.1109/mwc.2018.1700152
12. Kaleem, Z., et al.: Amateur drone surveillance: applications, architectures, enabling technologies, and public safety issues: Part 2. IEEE Commun. Mag. **56**(4), 66–67 (2018)
13. Khan, F.R., et al.: A cost-efficient autonomous air defense system for national security. Secur. Commun. Netw. **2021**, 1–10 (2021). https://doi.org/10.1155/2021/9984453
14. Krizhevsky, A., Sutskever, I., Hinton, G.E.: Imagenet classification with deep convolutional neural networks. Commun. ACM **60**(6), 84–90 (2017). https://doi.org/10.1145/3065386

15. Liu, B., Luo, H.: An improved YOLOv5 for multi-rotor UAV detection. Electronics **11**(15), 2330 (2022). https://doi.org/10.3390/electronics11152330

16. Liu, H., Fan, K., Ouyang, Q., Li, N.: Real-time small drones detection based on pruned YOLOv4. Sensors **21**(10), 3374 (2021). https://doi.org/10.3390/s21103374

17. Mahdavi, F., Rajabi, R.: Drone detection using convolutional neural networks. In: 2020 6th Iranian Conference on Signal Processing and Intelligent Systems (ICSPIS) (2020). https://doi.org/10.1109/icspis51611.2020.9349620

18. Mittal, U., Srivastava, S., Chawla, P.: Object detection and classification from thermal images using region based convolutional neural network. J. Comput. Sci. **15**(7), 961–971 (2019). https://doi.org/10.3844/jcssp.2019.961.971

19. Ng, L.S., Yusoff, W.A., Dhinesh, R., Sak, J.S.: Low cost night vision system for intruder detection. IOP Conf. Ser. Mater. Sci. Eng. **114**, 012139 (2016). https://doi.org/10.1088/1757-899x/114/1/012139

20. Redmon, J., Divvala, S., Girshick, R., Farhadi, A.: You only look once: unified, real-time object detection. In: 2016 IEEE Conference on Computer Vision and Pattern Recognition (CVPR) (2016). DOI: https://doi.org/10.1109/cvpr.2016.91

21. Ren, S., He, K., Girshick, R., Sun, J.: Faster R-CNN: towards real-time object detection with region proposal networks. IEEE Trans. Pattern Anal. Mach. Intell. **39**(6), 1137–1149 (2017). https://doi.org/10.1109/tpami.2016.2577031

22. Rodin, C.D., de Lima, L.N., de Alcantara Andrade, F.A., Haddad, D.B., Johansen, T.A., Storvold, R.: Object classification in thermal images using convolutional neural networks for search and rescue missions with unmanned aerial systems. In: 2018 International Joint Conference on Neural Networks (IJCNN) (2018). https://doi.org/10.1109/ijcnn.2018.8489465

23. Samadzadegan, F., Dadrass Javan, F., Ashtari Mahini, F., Gholamshahi, M.: Detection and recognition of drones based on a deep convolutional neural network using visible imagery. Aerospace **9**(1), 31 (2022). https://doi.org/10.3390/aerospace9010031

24. Schumann, A., Sommer, L., Klatte, J., Schuchert, T., Beyerer, J.: Deep cross-domain flying object classification for robust UAV detection. In: 2017 14th IEEE International Conference on Advanced Video and Signal Based Surveillance (AVSS) (2017). https://doi.org/10.1109/avss.2017.8078558

25. Seidaliyeva, U., Akhmetov, D., Ilipbayeva, L., Matson, E.T.: Real-time and accurate drone detection in a video with a static background. Sensors **20**(14), 3856 (2020). https://doi.org/10.3390/s20143856

26. Shakoor, S., Kaleem, Z., Baig, M.I., Chughtai, O., Duong, T.Q., Nguyen, L.D.: Role of UAVs in public safety communications: energy efficiency perspective. IEEE Access **7**, 140665–140679 (2019)

27. Shi, Q., Li, J.: Objects detection of UAV for anti-UAV based on YOLOv4. In: 2020 IEEE 2nd International Conference on Civil Aviation Safety and Information Technology (ICCASIT (2020). https://doi.org/10.1109/iccasit50869.2020.9368788

28. Svanstrom, F., Englund, C., Alonso-Fernandez, F.: Real-time drone detection and tracking with visible, thermal and acoustic sensors. In: 2020 25th International Conference on Pattern Recognition (ICPR) (2021). https://doi.org/10.1109/icpr48806.2021.9413241

29. Szegedy, C., Toshev, A., Erhan, D.: Deep neural networks for object detection. In: Advances in Neural Information Processing Systems, vol. 26 (2013)

30. Virasova, A., Klimov, D., Khromov, O., Gubaidullin, I., Oreshko, V.: Rich feature hierarchies for accurate object detection and semantic segmentation. Radioengineering, 115–126 (2021). https://doi.org/10.18127/j00338486-202109-11

31. Xu, W., Yang, Z., Ng, D.W.K., Levorato, M., Eldar, Y.C., et al.: Edge learning for B5G networks with distributed signal processing: semantic communication, edge computing, and wireless sensing. arXiv preprint arXiv:2206.00422 (2022)
32. Yang, Z., Chen, M., Saad, W., Hong, C.S., Shikh-Bahaei, M.: Energy efficient federated learning over wireless communication networks. IEEE Trans. Wirel. Commun. **20**(3), 1935–1949 (2020)

Study on Detection of Vascular Inner Wall with IVUS Image

Hangxu Su, Lvming Lv, Xufen Xie, and Miao Miao[✉]

School of Information Science and Engineering, Dalian Polytechnic University, NO. 1
Qinggongyuan, Ganjingzi District, Dalian 116034, China
h9655631160@163.com, miaomiao@dlpu.edu.cn

Abstract. Images obtained by Intravascular ultrasound (IVUS) technology play
a key role in detecting the lining of blood vessels. However, IVUS images are not
clear enough usually, it is difficult to detect the inner wall of the blood vessels. It
further affects the diagnosis results. In view of this situation, we first applies the
pseudo-color enhancement algorithm to enhance the image; Second, the images
were dichotomized by Support Vector Classification (SVC), and the images were
divided into internal and external parts; then Hough gradient transform based on
Canny operator is applied to detect the inner wall of blood vessels. The proposed
method was applied to detect 100 frames of IVUS images and compared with the
actual judgment results of doctors. The detection results showed that the detection
results of blood vessel lining in 97 frames were consistent with the doctors' judgment results, and the detection accuracy could reach 97%. Experimental results
show that the method can effectively highlight the characteristics of the inner wall
of blood vessels and detect the inner wall of blood vessels. It can greatly improve
the diagnostic accuracy in the actual medical process.

Keywords: IVUS · SVC · False color enhancement · Detection of blood vessel
lining

1 Literature Review

Due to its convenience, noninvasive and flexible features, IVUS technology has been
playing a high role in vascular diagnosis in recent years. However, because the recognition result image of this technology is visually presented as gray image, it is not clear
enough, difficult to identify and other characteristics, which has played a great obstacle
to doctors' medical diagnosis [1–7].

Current studies on the detection of vascular inner wall with IVUS images can be
seen as follows: In 2012, aiming at the detection problem of IVUS images, Li Yilin et al.
from Beijing University of Technology proposed to use grayscale co-occurrence matrix
and grayscale gradient co-occurrence matrix to extract image eigenvalues, and then
designed Support Vector Machine (SVM) classifier to train and classify the extracted
eigenvalues. Cross Validation method (CV) was used to evaluate the results, which was

J. Zhao (Ed.): WiSATS 2023, LNICST 509, pp. 19–30, 2023.
https://doi.org/10.1007/978-3-031-34851-8_2

characterized by excessive computation and complicated processing [8]. In 2018, Yuan Shaofeng et al. from Southern University of Science and Technology used the deep full convolutional network (DFCN) model to process the original IVUS image, and then used the shape information of the inner wall of the blood vessel to reduce the influence of the wrong pixels, and finally carried out the image segmentation operation. The calculation process of the model is complicated and difficult to achieve in the actual medical diagnosis process [9]. In 2018, Wu Yupeng et al. from South China University of Technology proposed to use three network models based on U-Net, Dense-U-Net and Res-U-Net to, segment the studied area in the intima of blood vessels, and then establish deep learning models for lipid, fiber and calcified plaques respectively. This model needs to be further strengthened in three aspects: sample data adoption, model optimization and clinical application [10]. In 2021, Zhang Wenzhen et al. from Shandong University took U-net as the network framework and used active contour model, edge operator and K-means clustering algorithm to build a segmentation model for IVUS image. This model can simplify doctors' diagnosis and treatment process and provide data support. However, the scale of its data set is small and the model generalization ability is weak [11]. In 2021, Li Kai et al. from Zhejiang University of Science and Technology constructed an automatic detection model of vascular intima boundary in IVUS images. This model combined artificial features and higher-order semantic features, screened out the most featured data subset through improved cuckoo search, and input it into the dictionary for the classification and boundary detection of vascular inner wall. The self-comparison experiment proved that the recognition accuracy and effectiveness of the model were significantly improved, but the method was too complicated [12]. In 2018, Huang Zhijie et al. from Southern Medical University firstly adopted filtering binary processing for the original IVUS image. After more image texture features are obtained, the IVUS images are classified by linear classifier, random forest and other classification methods. Experimental results show that the recognition accuracy is greatly improved, but the processing process is complicated [13]. In 2011, Sun Zheng et al. from North China Electric Power University proposed a 3D parallel segmentation algorithm based on snake model. The algorithm firstly weakens the noise of the original image, so as to obtain the four longitudinal views of the IVUS image sequence. After extracting the divided boundaries, the boundary curve is mapped to obtain the initial contour in the view. Finally, the initial contour is used as the initial shape of the snake model. The boundary features of each frame IVUS image are obtained. The segmentation results of this method are not high in accuracy [14]. In 2016, Wang Ling et al. from Tianjin University obtained the local optimal solution of IVUS image segmentation by using dynamic programming algorithm, time-domain noise reduction preprocessing and active contour model. This method has good repeatability, high accuracy and stability, but the processing process is complex [15].

2 Introduction

In this paper, based on MATLAB and python language, aiming at the problem of low resolution of IVUS image, a new method for processing IVUS image is proposed. In this process, pseudo-color transformation is applied to enhance the original image of

IVUS. Then the appropriate kernel function is used to classify the image by support vector machine. Further, Hough gradient transform based on Canny operator was used to extract the range of the inner wall of the blood vessel to realize the detection process. The method was used to detect 100 frames of images, and compared with the actual judgment results of doctors. The results showed that 97 frames of images were consistent with the judgment results of doctors, and the recognition accuracy could reach 97%. It can be proved that the above method can improve the accuracy of diagnosis in the actual process of diagnosis and treatment.

3 Methods

In this paper, the original IVUS image processing, the first use of false color enhancement algorithm in MATLAB, the original IVUS image false color enhancement. By using python language, the key pixel points of the enhanced image were selected, and the support vector machine classification model was trained using the key pixel points, and the original image was segmented using the obtained model. The range of the inner wall of the blood vessel was obtained by gray scale transformation, median filtering, Canny operator edge detection and Hough gradient transformation for the segmented image, so as to realize the detection of the inner wall of the blood vessel. The specific scheme is shown in Fig. 1.

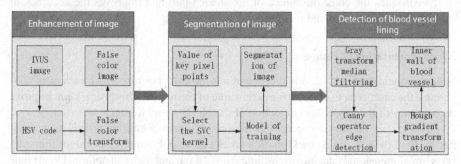

Fig. 1. Schematic diagram of the method

3.1 Enhancement of Image

Intravascular ultrasound (IVUS) is a kind of tomography technology. The obtained image is a gray image in human eye recognition, which has the characteristics of small brightness difference of pixels and is not easy to recognize. Therefore, this paper uses the pseudo-color enhancement algorithm to process the image, increase the computer's identification of the image, and improve the processing efficiency of the subsequent algorithm on the IVUS image.

Firstly, the mapping relationship between the three basic RGB colors and gray scale function $g(x, y)$ is established by constructing three color transfer functions $R(x, y)$,

$G(x, y)$ and $B(x, y)$. Then, the constructed color functions $R(x, y)$, $G(x, y)$ and $B(x, y)$ are linearly accumulated to achieve the purpose of image enhancement.

The relation between pixel value C of the pseudo-color image and the original IVUS image is shown in Formula (1):

$$C = R(x, y) + G(x, y) + B(x, y) \tag{1}$$

In the formula, $R(x, y)$, $G(x, y)$ and $B(x, y)$ are the three color transfer functions constructed respectively, and the formulas are (2), (3) and (4) as follows:

$$R(x, y) = \begin{cases} 0, & 0 \leq f(x, y) < 64; \\ 255(f(x, y) - 64)/64, & 64 \leq f(x, y) < 128; \\ 255, & 128 \leq f(x, y) < 256; \end{cases} \tag{2}$$

$$G(x, y) = \begin{cases} 0, & 0 \leq f(x, y) < 128; \\ 255(f(x, y) - 128)/96, & 128 \leq f(x, y) < 224; \\ 255, & 224 \leq f(x, y) < 256; \end{cases} \tag{3}$$

$$B(x, y) = \begin{cases} 255, & 0 \leq f(x, y) < 64; \\ 255(128 - f(x, y))/64 & 64 \leq f(x, y) < 128; \\ 0, & 128 \leq f(x, y) < 256; \end{cases} \tag{4}$$

The above process converts the original IVUS image into RGB false color image, which enhances the color difference of the shaded part and improves the accuracy of subsequent segmentation and recognition.

3.2 Segmentation of Image

Image segmentation is to divide the image into non-intersecting and meaningful sub-regions, the essence is to classify the pixel value of the image. This process can improve the accuracy of the subsequent detection of the blood vessel lining.

In this paper, the support vector machine classification algorithm is used to segment the image in python. The kernel function takes a cubic polynomial. This algorithm converts low-dimensional data into high-dimensional data, and seeks an optimal hyperplane that can separate the two types of key data in the high-dimensional space, so as to achieve the purpose of data set classification and segmentation. The processing process is shown in Fig. 2.

Before the segmentation operation, the segmentation samples to be processed are selected in advance. According to the doctor's guidance, 10 image key points and 10 segmentation target key points were artificially selected on the image after the pseudo-color enhancement processing in the previous step, and their RGB values were extracted. As shown in Fig. 3 and Fig. 4.

The extracted two sets of key points are converted into x vector and y vector respectively.

The cubic polynomial kernel function selected by the SVC model is shown in formula (5):

$$K(x, y) = [(x, y) + 1]^3 \tag{5}$$

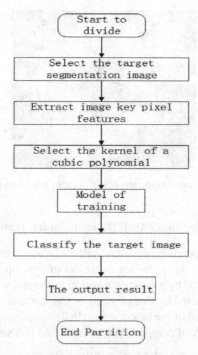

Fig. 2. SVM-based segmentation process

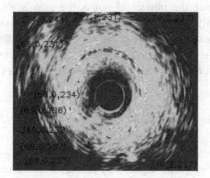

Fig. 3. Image key point value

The discriminant function of support vector machine construction is shown in Formula (6):

$$h(t) = sign\left\{ \sum_{i=1}^{s} \alpha_i y_i [(x, y) + 1]^3 - b \right\} \tag{6}$$

In the formula, s is the number of support vector machines; x and y are image key point vectors and segmentation target key point vectors respectively; i and b are constants.

After x vector and y vector are trained in the constructed SVC model, the model is used to predict and segment the whole original image, so as to get the segmtioned image.

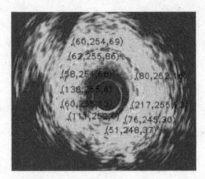

Fig. 4. The value of the target key point of image segmentation

3.3 Detection of Vascular Inner Wall Based on Hofer Transform

In order to simplify the operation, the inner wall of the actual blood vessel was approximately treated as a ring. After the segmentation of the enhanced IVUS image, the obtained image is processed by gray scale transformation and median filtering, and then the ring boundary is extracted by Hough gradient transformation based on Canny operator to detect the inner wall of the blood vessel. In this process, Hoff gradient transform can improve the efficiency of computer recognition, and it is simple and effective.

Grayscale Transformation and Median Filtering. Since image noise has a great impact on the edge detection process, before using Hough transform detection technology, in order to reduce the impact of noise, the gray scale transformation of the segmented image is firstly carried out. In addition, due to the complex imaging of the vascular image itself, the quality of the photo is poor, so the image should be processed by the median filtering, in order to perform the Hough transform more effectively.

The grayscale transformation formula is shown in Formula (7):

$$g(x, y) = \begin{cases} \frac{c}{a} f(x, y) & 0 \leq f(x, y) < a; \\ \frac{d-c}{b-c}[f(x, y) - a] + c & a \leq f(x, y) < b; \\ \frac{M_g - d}{M_f - b}[f(x, y) - b] + d & b \leq f(x, y) < M_f; \end{cases} \quad (7)$$

In the formula, $f(x, y)$ is the segmented image; a and b are the piecewise values of input image pixel brightness; c, d is the piecewise value of the output image pixel brightness; M_f and M_g are the maximum brightness values of input image and output image pixels respectively.

The median filtering processing formula is shown in Formula (8):

$$p(x, y) = Med_{(s,t) \in \varpi_{xy}} g(s, t) \quad (8)$$

In the formula, $p(x, y)$ is the image after median filtering; ϖ_{xy} is a square adjacent domain centered on points x and y; $g(s, t)$ is the input image.

Canny Edge Detection. Canny edge detection before Hough transformation can improve the accuracy of the value of the inner wall of the blood vessel. The essence of this algorithm is to find the pixels with the largest gradient amplitude change in the image and save the statistics. Canny edge detection steps are as follows:

The Image Pixel Value is Smoothed by Gaussian Filter to Eliminate Noise. The filter definition is shown in Formula (9):

$$T(x, y) = f(x, y) * H(x, y) \tag{9}$$

$$H(x, y) = \frac{1}{2\pi\sigma^2} e^{\frac{x^2+y^2}{2\delta^2}} \tag{10}$$

where, $f(x, y)$ is the original image; $T(x, y)$ is the output image; $H(x, y)$ is the Gaussian filter.

Calculate the Gradient and Direction of Amplitude. Let T_x and T_y be the row and column filters after smooth processing, and the expression is (11), (12) as shown below:

$$T_x = [f(x+1, y) - f(x, y) + f(x+1, y+1) - f(x, y+1)]/2 \tag{11}$$

$$T_y = [f(x, y+1) - f(x, y) + f(x+1, y+1) - f(x+1, y)]/2 \tag{12}$$

The amplitude $M(x, y)$ and azimuth $\theta(x, y)$ of the corresponding gradient can be calculated using the coordinate transformation relation. It is defined as formula (13), as shown in Formula (14):

$$M(x, y) = \sqrt{T_x(x, y)^2 + T_y(x, y)^2} \tag{13}$$

$$\theta(x, y) = \arctan(\frac{T_x(x, y)}{T_y(x, y)}) \tag{14}$$

Suppression of Non-maximum and Double Threshold Detection. The suppressed maximum value means that the maximum value of pixel gradient in each column of the image is reserved, while the other pixel gradient values are set to zero. This method can determine whether the current pixel is the maximum point of the surrounding pixel gradient, eliminate the adverse effects of edge detection, and find the local maximum position of the pixel through the direction. Double threshold detection is to first compare two fixed values with gradient values, then eliminate the pixels whose gradient value is less than the low threshold, and unify the pixels whose gradient value is greater than the high threshold into the high threshold, so as to determine the boundary range of the inner wall of the blood vessel.

Hough Gradient Transform Detection. After the Canny operator was used to detect the boundary of the bleeding tube wall in the previous step, Hough gradient transform was further used to confirm the geometric center and effective range of the vessel wall, and circled in the original image.

Introduction to Hough Gradient Transformation. Hough gradient transform is a circle detection method based on Hough circle transform. Based on the gradient direction of each edge point calculated by Canny edge detection algorithm in the previous step, the pixel points contained in each gradient direction line are voted, and the pixel points with the most voting times are defined as the geometric center of the image. Then, the number of distance occurrences from the center of the circle to the edge was summed up, and the distance with the largest number of occurrences was defined as the radius, and the range of the inner wall of the blood vessel was determined according to the obtained center and radius.

Hough Gradient Transformation Calculation Process. Since the inner wall of the blood vessel is approximated as a ring, its definition is shown in Formula (15):

$$(x - a)^2 + (y - b)^2 = r^2 \tag{15}$$

In the formula, a and b are the center of the circle in Cartesian coordinates; r is the radius of the circle.

By using Hough gradient method and using Sobel operator on the boundary of pipe wall detected by Canny algorithm, the gradient value can be obtained by calculating the first derivative of the direction for the determined non-zero point.

Sobel operator is defined as (16):

$$\nabla f(x, y) = \begin{bmatrix} G_x \\ G_y \end{bmatrix} = \begin{bmatrix} \dfrac{\partial f}{\partial x} & \dfrac{\partial f}{\partial y} \end{bmatrix}^T \tag{16}$$

In the formula, $\nabla f(x, y)$ represents the modulus of the gradient; $f(x, y)$ represents the function image to be processed.

The gradient modulus can be expressed by formula (17):

$$|\nabla f(x, y)| = \left[\left(\frac{\partial f}{\partial x} \right)^2 + \left(\frac{\partial f}{\partial y} \right)^2 \right]^{\frac{1}{2}} \tag{17}$$

The definition of gradient direction is shown in Eq. (18):

$$\alpha(x, y) = \arctan \left[\frac{G_y}{G_x} \right] \tag{18}$$

The corresponding line segment can be determined and its pixels saved by combining the gradient direction $\alpha(x, y)$ and the distance from the non-zero of the boundary. When more pixels are accumulated, that is, more line segments intersect the pixel, the point can be determined as the geometric center of the blood vessel wall, and the range of the blood vessel wall can be determined by combining with the ring boundary detected by the Canny operator.

4   Experiment and Results

In this paper, repeated experiments were carried out according to the above method, and a number of detection results were obtained. In order to verify the feasibility of this method, the statistical results were compared with the actual judgment results of doctors.

The results show that 97 frames can accurately identify the inner wall of blood vessels among the 100 frames processed by this algorithm, and the recognition accuracy can reach 97%. It is proved that the method in this paper can effectively identify the vascular wall, and the operation method is simple and easy. Part of the experimental results are shown in the figure below (Figs. 5, 6, 7 and 8):

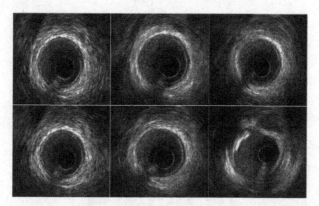

Fig. 5. Original image of IVUS

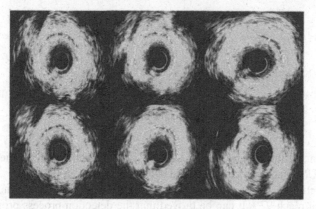

Fig. 6. IVUS enhanced image

The specific operation method for the accuracy verification of the model is as follows: Firstly, RGB values of 10 image key points and 10 segmentation target key points are selected respectively from 100 images after enhanced processing under the guidance of doctors, and they are taken as x vector and the y vector. Then, x vector and y vector are taken as parameters and put into the set SVC model for training, and the model after training is obtained. Then the trained model is used to predict and segment the original image, so as to get the segmented image. Then Hough gradient transformation was performed on the segmentation image to obtain the range of the inner wall of the blood vessel. The test results obtained by the method in this paper are compared with the actual judgment results of doctors to determine the validity of the model.

Fig. 7. IVUS segmentation image

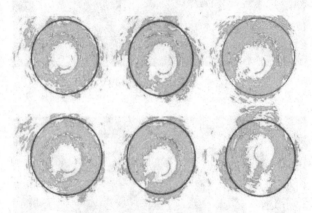

Fig. 8. IVUS Hough transform image

By comparing the experimental results, it can be seen that 97 frames of the 100 frames of IVUS images processed by the detection process in this paper are consistent with the detection results of doctors, and the detection accuracy of the model vascular inner wall can reach 97%.It can be proved that the detection process proposed in this paper can effectively identify the inner wall of blood vessels, effectively simplify the detection process in the actual medical process, and improve the detection accuracy of the inner wall of blood vessels.

To verify the stability of the detection algorithm in this paper. By changing the parameter configuration of Hough gradient transform function, the range of vascular inner wall in IVUS image was redetected. The minimum parameter of the circle radius of the detection function is increased by 10 each time from 1, and the maximum parameter of the circle radius is increased by 1000 each time to achieve this purpose. The running result is shown in Fig. 9.

As can be seen from Fig. 9, by changing the parameters of Hough gradient trans-formation function, there is no significant difference in the detected blood vessel inner wall. It can be proved that the detection algorithm has stability in the detection process.

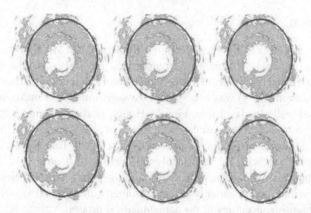

Fig. 9. Redetected IVUS images after adjusting detection function parameters

To verify the effectiveness of SVC segmentation algorithm proposed in this paper. The threshold segmentation method, region segmentation method and K-means segmentation method were successively applied to the IVUS image after pseudo-color transformation. By comparing different segmentation algorithms to generate different segmentation results, the validity of the segmentation algorithm in this paper is verified. The comparison of operation results of different segmentation algorithms is shown in Fig. 10.

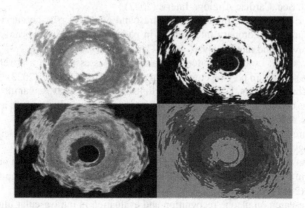

Fig.10. IVUS images segmented under different segmentation algorithms

It can be seen from Fig. 10 that the SVC segmentation algorithm proposed in this paper is relatively effective in predictive segmentation of images from the segmentation results obtained by using different segmentation algorithms.

5 Conclusion

This paper presents an IVUS image detection method based on MATLAB and python. In this method, the original IVUS image was transformed into a false-color image which was easier to be recognized by computer through false-color enhancement. Then, the Support Vector Classification (SVC) was used for image segmentation to make the contour of the blood vessel wall clearly visible. Finally, Hough gradient change based on Canny operator was used to detect the vascular wall image of IVUS image to achieve effective recognition. The above method was applied to detect 100 frames of IVUS original images, and compared with the actual judgment results of doctors. The experimental results show that this method can effectively highlight the characteristics of the inner wall of blood vessels and accurately detect the inner wall of blood vessels, which can improve the diagnostic accuracy in the actual medical process.

References

1. Qiao, G., Jiang, X., Dong, Z., Fu, W.: Application of intravascular ultrasound in the treatment of lower limb artery disease. Chin. J. Surg. **60**(12),1116–1120 (2022)
2. Dhara, S.S., Stines, I., Milner, R.: Intravascular ultrasound-guided transcaval approach for thoracic endovascular aneurysm repair. J. Vasc. Surg. Cases Innov. Tech. **8**(4) (2022)
3. Woong, R.J., et al.: Impact of intravascular ultrasound in acute myocardial infarction patients at high ischemic risk. Revista espanola de cardiologia (English edn.) (2022)
4. Cortese, B., Piraino, D., Gentile, D., Onea, H.L., Lazar, L.: Intravascular imaging for left main stem assessment: an update on the most recent clinical data. Catheterization Cardiovasc. Interv. Off. J. Soc. Cardiac Angiogr. Interv. (2022)
5. Groenland, F.T.W., et al.: Intravascular ultrasound-guided versus coronary angiography-guided percutaneous coronary intervention in patients with acute myocardial infarction: a systematic review and meta-analysis. Int. J. Cardiol. **353** (2022)
6. Zheng, J.-F., et al.: Long-term safety and absorption assessment of a novel bioresorbable nitrided iron scaffold in porcine coronary artery. Bioactive Mater. **17** (2022)
7. Zhong, Z., Zhao, L., Chen, K., Xia, S.: The clinical effects of intravascular ultrasound-guided percutaneous coronary intervention in patients with chronic total occlusion: a meta-analysis. Cardiol. Res. Pract. **2022** (2022)
8. Li, Y.: Research on artery plaque recognition method based on IVUS image. Beijing University of Technology (2012)
9. Yuan, S., Yang, F., Xu, L., Liu, S., Ji, F., Huang, J.: Detection of inner and outer membrane boundaries in IVUS images by deep full convolutional networks. J. Image Graph. **23**(09), 1335–1348 (2018)
10. Wu, Y.P.: Research on plaque recognition and evaluation in intravascular ultrasound image based on deep learning network. South China University of Technology (2018)
11. Zhang, W.Z.: Intelligent detection of coronary artery lesions based on intravascular ultrasound and its application. Shandong University (2021)
12. Li, K.: Cardiovascular intima of IVUS image edge detection algorithms. Zhejiang University of Technology (2021)
13. Huang, Z.J.: Study on the identification method of atherosclerotic plaque tissue area based on intravascular ultrasound image. Southern Medical University (2018)
14. Sun, Z., Yang, Y.: Three-dimensional IVUS image sequence segmentation method based on snake Model. J. Eng. Graph. **32**(06), 25–32 (2011)
15. Wang, L., Chen, X., Dong, F., Yang, G., Wang, F.: IVUS image sequence segmentation based on dynamic programming. J. Tianjin Univ. Technol. **32**(05), 16–20 (2016)

Anomaly Detection for Connected Autonomous Vehicles Using LSTM and Gaussian Naïve Bayes

Pegah Mansourian[1]([✉]) [iD], Ning Zhang[1] [iD], Arunita Jaekel[1] [iD],
Mina Zamanirafe[1], and Marc Kneppers[2]

[1] University of Windsor, Windsor, ON, Canada
mansourp@uwindsor.ca
[2] Telus Communications Inc., Vancouver, Canada

Abstract. In the foreseen future, connected autonomous vehicles (CAVs) are expected to improve driving safety and experience considerably; however, cybersecurity remains a critical issue. CAN protocol, the de-facto standard for in-vehicle networks, provides no security mechanism, which makes it one of the most attack-prone parts. The lack of security mechanisms in CAN messages allows intruders to conduct devastating attacks, putting drivers' and passengers' lives at risk. An Intrusion Detection System (IDS) can monitor CAN network activities and detect suspicious behaviors resulting from an attack to help safeguard CAVs. The destructive behavior of an intruder is reflected as point and group anomalies in the sequence of CAN messages. Our study proposes an LSTM-based IDS for the CAN bus by exploiting the temporal correlations of the messages on the bus to detect anomalies. Specifically, it is a one-class classifier trained with attack-free data to predict the upcoming value of CAN messages. Then a Gaussian Naïve Bayes classifier is used to classify messages as normal and attack according to the resulting prediction errors. The proposed IDS is evaluated in terms of detection performance and compared with state-of-the-art one-class classifiers, including OCSVM, Isolation Forest, and Autoencoder, using two real-world datasets (Car Hacking Dataset and Survival Analysis Dataset). The proposed method outperforms baselines and achieves detection accuracy and F-score by nearly 100%.

Keywords: In-vehicle security · CAN · Anomaly detection · IDS · LSTM

1 Introduction

Connected autonomous vehicles (CAVs) incorporating a variety of sensors and onboard computing, expect to significantly improve road safety and efficiency of the transportation system. A CAV can have over 100 Electronics Control Units (ECUs), which help achieve a certain level of automation and gain essential information for decision makings. ECUs can handle different tasks, ranging from simple operations such as opening a window to more critical complex ones that

J. Zhao (Ed.): WiSATS 2023, LNICST 509, pp. 31–43, 2023.
https://doi.org/10.1007/978-3-031-34851-8_3

need communication between several ECUs, such as line detection and adaptive cruise control. Therefore, for a vehicle to work properly, an in-vehicle communication network is required to exchange messages of the ECUs with each other and the gateway to the out-of-vehicle world [15]. There are several protocols designed for the in-vehicle network, including Local Interconnect Network(LIN), Media-Oriented System Transport(MOST), FlexRay, and Controller Area Network (CAN). MOST is an expensive and high-bandwidth protocol, mainly used for the infotainment system, while LIN is a low-bandwidth protocol used for non-safety critical sensors and actuators. However, CAN is the dominant in-vehicle protocol due to its simplicity and reliability.

While the introduction of CAV brings comfort and safety features, the addition of components like ECUs, their distributed internal communications, and external network access generate new attack surfaces and raise security issues. An attacker can gain access to the in-vehicle network either by exploiting an external wireless communication, for instance, Wi-Fi and Bluetooth, or by physically tapping into the CAN bus via OBD-II Port and causing critical damage to the vehicle, driver, and passengers [8]. For CAN bus, encryption, authentication, and other security measures are not supported. Due to the broadcast nature of the CAN bus, lack of authentication (sender ID) and encryption, and weak access control, CAN protocol is prone to many attacks, e.g., DoS, masquerade, suspension, replay, fabrication, and remote access attacks. In an experiment, Koscher et al. connected to the OBD-II port of a car and sniffed the packets on the CAN bus with the CARSHARK component. Then by targeted probing, fuzzy, and reverse engineering techniques, they could identify the corresponding messages of each ECU. They successfully overrode Body Control Module (BCM) messages of door locks, headlights, and wipers and displayed the manipulated speedometer readings on the Driver Information Center [8].

As there are no security mechanisms in the CAN protocol, the next defense layer is to deploy an intrusion detection system (IDS) in accordance with the defense-in-depth strategy. IDS is a system to monitor the events and messages in the network to detect malicious events and violations. Depending on the detection approach, IDS classifies into signature-based, anomaly-based, and hybrid IDS. In a signature-based IDS, every network traffic is checked against a database that contains signatures of known attacks to detect a match or intrusion. Signature-based IDS are incapable of detecting unknown types of attacks or zero-day attacks. Anomaly-based IDS, on the other hand, can accomplish this goal by obtaining the expected profile of the network and detecting deviations from it as intrusions. It is more common these days because of the ability to work well with rarely available attack data and independently of human knowledge. Some anomaly-based IDS use the statistical [12, 16] or information theory [13] features of CAN messages to identify anomalies, while others offer machine learning methods like SVM [1, 2, 18], HMM [9, 14], SOM [3], GBDT [19], and NN [4, 6, 7, 10, 11, 17, 20].

In this paper, we propose an anomaly-based IDS for the CAN bus network by using machine learning. Attacks on the CAN bus are group (conditional) anomalies and only can be identified when examining them in a batch of data.

Hence in the proposed IDS, an LSTM module is designed to extract the normal model of the CAN network, considering the sequence of messages in time. It uses the latest historical CAN messages as input and predicts the current expected message based on them. Conditional anomalies in CAN messages can be reduced to point anomalies considering LSTM prediction errors, which can then be classified using conventional machine learning techniques. Unless an attack is conducted, the predicted value accords with the given value. When it comes to the attack case, the prediction errors raise the alarm about suspicious activity. In our experiments, we have found that the prediction errors produced by the attack and normal classes data follow Normal or Gaussian distributions with different mean and standard deviations. Among classifiers, the Gaussian Naïve Bayes (GNB) classifier focuses on the difference between Gaussian distributions of features across classes. Therefore, we have combined the LSTM module with a GNB classifier to find point anomalies in the prediction errors.

In the rest of the paper, first, we review the previous studies on CAN bus anomaly detection-based IDS in Sect. 2 and categorize them according to their methodologies. Section 3 describes the overall structure of the proposed LSTM-GNB method and each building block in detail. In Sect. 4, two datasets are used to conduct experiments, and the performance evaluation results and comparisons with the state-of-the-art baselines are provided. Finally, the conclusion is outlined in Sect. 5.

2   Related Works

The security of In-vehicle networks, especially the CAN bus, is one of the challenging research areas. Different approaches are proposed by researchers to detect attacks on the CAN bus. The detection methods can be categorized into statistical-based, information theory-based, and machine-learning-based methods.

In the entropy-based anomaly detection proposed by Muter et al., it is assumed that the entropy in the normal activity of the network is low. Once an attack happens it changes the frequency and content of messages in a way that the entropy would increase in the network. They calculated the entropy at each time step t and compared it to the normal situation to find the attacks. They evaluated their method on a real vehicle connecting its CAN-Body to a laptop and logging the messages with CANoe software. In experiments, replay, flooding, and spoofing attack messages were injected, and their entropy-based method almost successfully detected them. However, it has a limitation on finding spoofed messages that adhere to the normal one [13].

Since in-vehicle networks are more restricted and deterministic than other types of networks, Taylor et al. proposed a statistical-based method that makes use of the frequency and timing feature of CAN messages in a moving window. Then it analyzes them with statistical formulas to extract the normal profile of the network and detect messages that violate the normal profile as anomalies. They also used a 2011 Ford Explorer to generate CAN messages and injected replay data into it with different rates and durations. The detection results were compared with OCSVM considering the Area Under Curve (AUC) metric. Despite the finding that AUC improves with increases in duration and rate, low-frequency and short-duration attacks might not be detected. [16].

The work done by Marchetti et al. is also a statistical anomaly detection. In this research, the authors model the normal behavior of the CAN bus by keeping track of all possible CAN ID sequences in a data structure called the transition matrix. In the detection phase, if an observed sequence of IDs does not match the transition matrix, it is labeled as an anomaly. Their method worked well with spoofed messages, reaching 100% detection, but very poor on replay messages since they were already seen in the attack-free data used in the training phase [12].

Although statistical and entropy-based approaches are very light-weighted and resource-friendly, they might fail to detect unseen (zero-day) attacks, especially when occurring within the content of messages. To overcome this challenge, machine learning has become the dominant approach to solving problems in unknown environments, where prior expert knowledge is not required to define patterns and features of the system. It has been widely used in recent studies done in the CAN bus anomaly detection area. Among machine learning-based methods, some of them are designed with conventional ML methods. The most popular conventional algorithms are SVM [1,2,18], HMM [9,14], SOM [3], and GBDT [19].

The neural network has shown good performance in recent studies on CAN bus anomaly detection. Kang et al. proposed a DNN structure to detect attacks in the CAN bus. To prevent the vanishing gradient problem in DNN, Restricted Boltzmann Machine is used to pre-train the model's weights. They evaluated their method on a simulated dataset generated by OCTANE and reached a 99.9 percent detection rate with seven hidden layers deep network [7].

A denoising autoencoder with a deep neural network structure is proposed by Lin et al. The model is trained with normal data; hence the anomalies cannot be reconstructed perfectly, and the error would raise an anomaly flag. The other novelty of their work is that they have used an evolutionary optimization algorithm to determine the best structure of the network in terms of the number and size of hidden layers. Three datasets were used to test the performance of this model - two generated and one publicly available OTIDS dataset. It is compared to ANN, K-means, and Decision Tree in terms of precision, recall, and F-score and achieved around 0.98 F-score, which is higher than the baselines [10].

Javed et al. designed an IDS for CAN, called CANintelliIDS. Their principal purpose is to utilize the correlation of data from multiple ECUs to improve detection performance. To this end, they have applied a neural network consisting of two layers of CNN followed by the GRU layer on a continuous flow of CAN messages. The proposed method has shown higher detection performance, around 93% F-score, compared to conventional ML and pure CNN, over OTIDS dataset [6].

Considering the fact that a temporal correlation exists in the messages exchanged on the CAN bus, Taylor et al. introduced LSTM into the network structure. The model predicts the next expected DATA payload for each ECU separately, and the aggregated bit log loss error over the whole word is used for detecting anomalies. By doing so, they could achieve approximately 0.99 AUC on most of the CAN IDs, tested on data collected from a 2012 Subaru Impreza with five types of anomalies: interleave, drop, discontinuity, unusual, and reverse [17].

LSTM is also used by Zhu et al. for anomaly detection. They have distributed the LSTM training on edge devices to reduce the response time and computation power [20]. Longari et al. proposed an LSTM-based Autoencoder as an unsupervised method, called CANnolo, to detect anomalies of independent ECUs and validated it by their own generated CAN message dataset [11]. In the CANet proposed by Hanselmann et al., the LSTM predictions of separate ECUs are reconstructed by feeding into an autoencoder to take the correlation of ECUs into account as well [4].

3   Proposed Method

Each ECU connected to the CAN bus periodically broadcasts measured data in CAN messages. As seen from Fig. 1, the content of messages generated by each ECU is correlate over time. The payload of transmitted messages at each time is affected by the flow of previous message payloads. This observation leads us to use LSTM units in our proposed anomaly detection method.

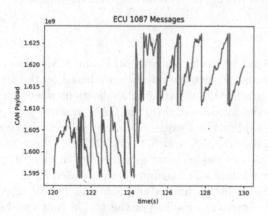

Fig. 1. A snapshot of the CAN message data contents over ten seconds period in the Car Hacking Dataset.

The complete structure of the proposed method is depicted in Fig. 2. It consists of three modules: LSTM network, prediction error calculator, and Gaussian Naïve Bayes (GNB) classifier. The input to our IDS is a 3D vector of integer data in the shape of (#samples, #lookback, #features), and the output is the probability of samples belonging to two classes of normal activities and attack. We will discuss each module in detail.

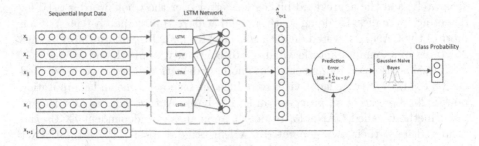

Fig. 2. The overall structure of the proposed LSTM-GNB IDS method.

3.1 Input Data

The input layer is fed with a sequence of data - the length of it is called lookback. We have removed additional features like arbitration ID and timestamp from the dataset and kept nine other features of CAN messages, including the Data Length Control (DLC) and eight bytes of payload as the data. To convert the raw data into the sequence format required by LSTM, we performed a moving window on the data to cut the data into sequential samples.

3.2 LSTM Network

Non-recurrent neural networks, such as MLP and CNN, do not have memory in their structure and predict the output only based on the given input at the current time. So, it is hard to use them in applications where data has sequential and temporal properties. In our case, the CAN message payload generated by an ECU can be considered in a sequence, and its value varies based on the previous observations. Recurrent Neural Network, RNN for short, offers the required ability, by introducing a hidden state as a memory in its structure, to maintain a history of observed data and make predictions based on it.

LSTM, introduced by Hochreiter and Schmidhuber [5], is an enhanced version of RNN. The internal structure of the LSTM unit can be seen in Fig. 3. The improvement involves solving the vanishing gradient problem of RNN by changing the learning strategy from learning what information to remember to learning what information to forget. To do so, three learnable gates in the LSTM structure control the hidden state to remember or forget information flow. First, the forget gate determines how much of the past information should be omitted. Second, the input gate controls the amount of data flow from current input x_t and cell state c_t based on their importance. Third, the output gate tunes how much the unit's current state is outputted. Assuming that i_t, f_t, o_t, c_t, and h_t

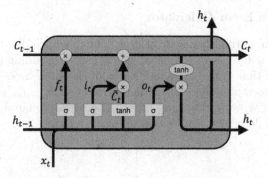

Fig. 3. Internal structure of LSTM unit.

denote the input gate, forget gate, output gate, cell state, and hidden state at timestep t, respectively, the mathematical working structure of LSTM can be calculated as:

$$i_t = \sigma(W_{xi}x_t + W_{hi}h_{t-1} + W_{ci} \odot C_{t-1} + b_i)$$
$$f_t = \sigma(W_{xf}x_t + W_{hf}h_{t-1} + W_{cf} \odot C_{t-1} + b_f)$$
$$C_t = f_t \odot C_{t-1} + i_t \odot \tanh(W_{xc}x_t + W_{hc}h_{t-1} + b_c) \qquad (1)$$
$$o_t = \sigma(W_{xo}x_t + W_{ho}h_{t-1} + W_{co} \odot C_t + b_o)$$
$$h_t = o_t \odot \tanh(C_t).$$

In Eq. 1, $W_h = \begin{pmatrix} W_{hi} \\ W_{hf} \\ W_{hc} \\ W_{ho} \end{pmatrix} \in \mathbb{R}^{\mathrm{dh} \times 4\mathrm{dh}}$ is hidden-to-hidden weight matrix, $W_x =$

$\begin{pmatrix} W_{xi} \\ W_{xf} \\ W_{xc} \\ W_{xo} \end{pmatrix} \in \mathbb{R}^{\mathrm{dx} \times 4\mathrm{dh}}$ is input-to-hidden weight matrix, $b = \begin{pmatrix} b_i \\ b_f \\ b_c \\ b_o \end{pmatrix} \in \mathbb{R}^{4\mathrm{dh}}$ is the

bias, and $C_0, h_0 \in \mathbb{R}^{4\mathrm{dh}}$ are the initial value of cell state and hidden state, respectively. Also, $\sigma(.)$ denotes the sigmoid activation function and $\odot$ is the Hadamard product operator.

The LSTM network consists of one LSTM layer and one Dense layer. It extracts the temporal features in the flow of messages in the learning phase and then predicts the expected value of the CAN payload based on the extracted features in the detection phase. The hidden LSTM layer, consisting of 32 units and the tanh activation function, performs the temporal correlation extraction. It is followed by a dense fully-connected output layer with nine neurons, each outputting one predicted feature of data.

The LSTM network is trained only with attack-free CAN messages to extract a model of an in-vehicle network operating normally. Using the ADAM optimizer, the MSE metric, and a learning rate of 0.001, the optimization is performed. The early stop method is implemented to avoid overfitting. Following ten epochs of training, if the trained model fails to improve on the validation data, the training is terminated.

3.3   Prediction Error Calculator

After learning the normal behavior of ECU, the model can be used to differentiate the normal and attack data based on their corresponding prediction error. At each point of time t, the expected status of the ECU message is predicted, denoted by $\hat{x}_t$, based on a sequence of historical data $[x_{t-lookback}, \ldots, x_{t-2}, x_{t-1}]$ given to the LSTM network as the input. The Mean Squared Error (MSE) is used in this module, which can be defined as:

$$MSE = \|x_t - \hat{x}_t\|. \tag{2}$$

The measured prediction error indicates how close the prediction of the LSTM network is to the currently observed value of the CAN message. Since the forecast is according to the normal profile of the network, it tends to be nearly zero for unmodified messages.

3.4   GNB Classifier

In the case of anomaly, the distribution of prediction error would be a Gaussian distribution with different parameters compared to the normal case. According to this observation, we have proposed to use a Gaussian Naïve Bayes classifier on the prediction errors to classify them into two classes of normal and attack data.

A Gaussian Naïve Bayes (GNB) classifier is integrated into the proposed IDS to classify messages based on the prediction error. GNB is an extension of the Naïve Bayes classifier, assuming the real-valued input data has Gaussian distribution with different parameters in different classes. It is a simple yet powerful classifier.

Having $p(C|H)$ as the conditional probability of data belonging to class C by considering hypothesis H and $p(C)$ and $p(H)$ as prior probability of class C and hypothesis H, the Bayes' theorem is stated as:

$$p(H|C) = \frac{p(C|H)p(H)}{p(C)}, \tag{3}$$

where $p(H|C)$ is the posterior probability and indicates the probability of hypothesis H given the class C data. The GNB makes use of Bayes' theorem to calculate the posterior probability of all possible hypotheses based on the prior possibilities, derived from given input data, and choose the one that maximizes the likelihood.

If an attacker injects or drops a message, the sequence of data does not follow the normal profile of the network and the LSTM module fails to predict it perfectly. As a result, if taking a look into the distribution of the prediction errors, the attack and normal data follow different Gaussian distributions. Figure 4 shows an example of prediction error distribution of two different features, using by LSTM module on data of one ECU.

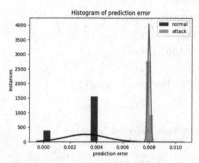 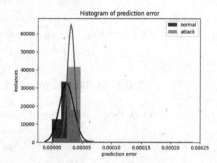

Fig. 4. Prediction error distribution of normal and attack CAN messages and their corresponding Gaussian distribution for two different features.

The GNB classifier module generates the final output, which is the probability of the input sample x_t belonging to classes of normal or attack. Our method selects the class with a higher probability and outputs it. If the observed CAN message is identified as malicious, our IDS will raise the alarm and notify the driver and the manufacturing company.

4   Performance Evaluation

This section discusses the experiments performed to evaluate the efficiency of our proposed LSTM-GNB IDS. Two datasets used for the evaluation are described first, followed by the evaluation procedure and the results.

4.1   Dataset

To evaluate our proposed method, we have made use of two datasets publicly available for CAN bus: Car Hacking Dataset and Survival Analysis Dataset for automobile IDS. The Car Hacking dataset is gathered by connecting two Raspberry Pi devices to the OBD-II port of a real car, one for logging the network traffic and one for injecting fabricated messages to the CAN bus. Four types of attacks, including DoS, fuzzy, RPM gauge, and gear spoofing, are implemented in this dataset. Each message in the data samples consists of a timestamp, CAN ID, DLC, DATA [0-7], and a flag indicating normal (R) or attack data (T).

The other dataset, Survival Analysis Dataset for automobile IDS, contains CAN bus messages of three cars from different vendors: Sonata, Spark, and Soul. For each vehicle, three attacks are performed and logged: Flooding, Fuzzy, and Malfunctioning. The structure of the data is similar to the Car Hacking Dataset. The summary of both datasets is given in Tables 1 and 2.

Table 1. The summary of Survival Analysis Dataset for automobile IDS.

Attack Type	Number of Messages		
	Sonata	Soul	Spark
Flooding	149,547	181,901	120,570
Fuzzy	135,670	249,990	65,665
Malfunction	132,651	173,436	79,787
Attack-Free	117,173	192,516	136,934

Table 2. The summary of the Car Hacking Dataset.

Attack type	Number of Messages		
	Total	Normal Messages	Injected Messages
Normal	988,987	988,987	0
DoS Attack	3,665,771	3,078,250	587,521
Fuzzy Attack	3,838,860	3,347,013	491,847
Gear Spoofing	4,443,142	3,845,890	597,252
RPM Spoofing	4,621,702	3,966,805	654,897

4.2 Results

Several experiments are conducted to evaluate the proposed method and compare it to other baselines. The Keras framework with the backend of Tensorflow is used to build and train the models, on a computer with 16 GB RAM and a Core i7 processor.

Each dataset consists of normal and attacks data files. The normal data is used to train and validate the LSTM network. The other datasets are split into two parts. Twenty percent of them are used to train the GNB, and the rest are fed into the network as test data to evaluate the performance of our method. In addition, the hyperparameters associated with the model are tuned by the grid search method to achieve the highest performance.

Attacks on the CAN bus rarely occur, while the majority of CAN messages represent the normal operation of the vehicle. As a result, the labeled data collected from the CAN bus forms an imbalanced dataset with the anomaly data as the minority class or outliers. Traditional classification algorithms fail in the imbalanced data case and tend to bias toward the overabundant subclass. However, some One Class Classification (OCC) algorithms can deal with imbalanced data. Based on this, the efficiency of our proposed approach was compared to some OCC approaches as a baseline. The baseline includes two one-class conventional classification methods, OCSVM (One-Class Support Vector Machines) with Stochastic Gradient Descent (SGD) and Isolation Forest, as well as a neural network-based method called LSTM Autoencoder. A comparison between the performance of the proposed LSTM-GNB IDS and baselines is given in Table 3.

Table 3. Comparison of proposed LSTM-GNB IDS with Baseline results on the Car Hacking Dataset.

Attack Types	Baseline Methods	Recall	Precision	F-Score	Accuracy
DoS	OCSVM	1.000	0.835	0.910	0.968
	Isolation Forest	1.000	0.718	0.836	0.937
	LSTM-AE	1.000	1.000	1.000	1.000
	LSTM-GNB	**1.000**	**1.000**	**1.000**	**1.000**
Fuzzy	OCSVM	0.987	0.793	0.879	0.965
	Isolation Forest	0.994	0.621	0.764	0.921
	LSTM-AE	0.998	0.977	0.987	0.989
	LSTM-GNB	**1.000**	**0.994**	**0.997**	**0.998**
Gear Spoofing	OCSVM	0 (TP = 0)	0	–	0.833
	Isolation Forest	0 (TP = 0)	0	–	0.835
	LSTM-AE	0.984	0.894	0.937	0.982
	LSTM-GNB	**1.000**	**1.000**	**1.000**	**1.000**
RPM Spoofing	OCSVM	0 (TP = 0)	0	–	0.826
	Isolation Forest	0 (TP = 0)	0	–	0.834
	LSTM-AE	0.995	0.893	0.987	0.982
	LSTM-GNB	**1.000**	**1.000**	**1.000**	**1.000**

Table 4. LSTM-GNB results on the Survival Analysis Dataset.

Attack Types	Baseline Methods	Recall	Precision	F-Score	Accuracy
Flooding	Spark	1.000	1.000	1.000	1.000
	Soul	1.000	1.000	1.000	1.000
	Sonata	1.000	1.000	1.000	1.000
Malfunction	Spark	1.000	1.000	1.000	1.000
	Soul	0.984	1.000	0.992	0.999
	Sonata	1.000	1.000	1.000	1.000
Fuzzy	Spark	0.996	0.997	0.997	0.998
	Soul	0.994	1.000	0.997	0.997
	Sonata	0.996	1.000	0.998	0.998

The Survival Analysis Dataset for automobile IDS consists of normal and attack data gathered from three different car vendors, Sonata, Spark, and Soul. The results on this dataset are shown in Table 4.

As can be seen from the results, our proposed method outperforms the baselines. OCSVM and Isolation Forest fail to detect spoofing attacks. It is because anomalies that happen in the spoofing attack are not point anomalies, but contextual anomalies. Individually, they can be the same as normal data instances and cannot be found by comparing them. However, they are anomalous when happening in the wrong position in a sequence of data points. The ability of our LSTM model to consider each data in a sequence boosts its detection performance.

The other observation from the results is that in both datasets, fuzzy attacks are the hardest type to be detected. In this type of attack, random messages with random IDs are injected into the network. This results in declaring some normal data as an anomaly by mistake and increased false alarms. However, the false positive rate is yet low enough compared to the baseline.

5   Conclusion

In this work, an anomaly-based IDS is proposed to detect attacks on the in-vehicle CAN bus. The proposed method consists of an LSTM trained with normal CAN messages to extract the usual sequential behavior of each ECU. The trained network is used to predict the next expected payload of ECU based on past observations and compare it to the current received value from ECU. The idea behind the proposed method is that when an attack happens, the trained LSTM network will fail to predict correctly, thus the prediction error is higher than normal. To classify them based on the prediction error a GNB classifier is used in the method. The performance of our anomaly detector is evaluated against three one-class classifiers, using two datasets. The results show that our method yields better performance than the baselines, due to its ability to consider the position of messages of each ECU in a time sequence, not individually, and extract more meaningful correlations.

References

1. Al-Saud, M., Eltamaly, A.M., Mohamed, M.A., Kavousi-Fard, A.: An intelligent data-driven model to secure intravehicle communications based on machine learning. IEEE Trans. Industr. Electron. **67**(6), 5112–5119 (2019)
2. Avatefipour, O., et al.: An intelligent secured framework for cyberattack detection in electric vehicles' can bus using machine learning. IEEE Access **7**, 127580–127592 (2019)
3. Barletta, V.S., Caivano, D., Nannavecchia, A., Scalera, M.: Intrusion detection for in-vehicle communication networks: an unsupervised Kohonen Som approach. Future Internet **12**(7), 119 (2020)
4. Hanselmann, M., Strauss, T., Dormann, K., Ulmer, H.: Canet: an unsupervised intrusion detection system for high dimensional can bus data. IEEE Access **8**, 58194–58205 (2020)
5. Hochreiter, S., Schmidhuber, J.: Long short-term memory. Neural Comput. **9**(8), 1735–1780 (1997)
6. Javed, A.R., Ur Rehman, S., Khan, M.U., Alazab, M., Reddy, T.: Canintelliids: detecting in-vehicle intrusion attacks on a controller area network using CNN and attention-based GRU. IEEE Trans. Netw. Sci. Eng. **8**(2), 1456–1466 (2021)
7. Kang, M.J., Kang, J.W.: A novel intrusion detection method using deep neural network for in-vehicle network security. In: 2016 IEEE 83rd Vehicular Technology Conference (VTC Spring), pp. 1–5. IEEE (2016)
8. Koscher, K., et al.: Experimental security analysis of a modern automobile. In: 2010 IEEE Symposium on Security and Privacy, pp. 447–462. IEEE (2010)

9. Levi, M., Allouche, Y., Kontorovich, A.: Advanced analytics for connected car cybersecurity. In: 2018 IEEE 87th Vehicular Technology Conference (VTC Spring), pp. 1–7. IEEE (2018)

10. Lin, Y., Chen, C., Xiao, F., Avatefipour, O., Alsubhi, K., Yunianta, A.: An evolutionary deep learning anomaly detection framework for in-vehicle networks-can bus. IEEE Trans. Ind. Appl. (2020)

11. Longari, S., Valcarcel, D.H.N., Zago, M., Carminati, M., Zanero, S.: Cannolo: an anomaly detection system based on LSTM autoencoders for controller area network. IEEE Trans. Netw. Serv. Manag. **18**(2), 1913–1924 (2020)

12. Marchetti, M., Stabili, D.: Anomaly detection of can bus messages through analysis of id sequences. In: 2017 IEEE Intelligent Vehicles Symposium (IV), pp. 1577–1583. IEEE (2017)

13. Müter, M., Asaj, N.: Entropy-based anomaly detection for in-vehicle networks. In: 2011 IEEE Intelligent Vehicles Symposium (IV), pp. 1110–1115. IEEE (2011)

14. Narayanan, S.N., Mittal, S., Joshi, A.: Obd_securealert: an anomaly detection system for vehicles. In: 2016 IEEE International Conference on Smart Computing (SMARTCOMP), pp. 1–6. IEEE (2016)

15. Nilsson, D.K., Phung, P.H., Larson, U.E.: Vehicle ECU classification based on safety-security characteristics. In: IET Road Transport Information and Control-RTIC 2008 and ITS United Kingdom Members' Conference, pp. 1–7. IET (2008)

16. Taylor, A., Japkowicz, N., Leblanc, S.: Frequency-based anomaly detection for the automotive can bus. In: 2015 World Congress on Industrial Control Systems Security (WCICSS), pp. 45–49. IEEE (2015)

17. Taylor, A., Leblanc, S., Japkowicz, N.: Anomaly detection in automobile control network data with long short-term memory networks. In: 2016 IEEE International Conference on Data Science and Advanced Analytics (DSAA), pp. 130–139. IEEE (2016)

18. Theissler, A.: Anomaly detection in recordings from in-vehicle networks. Big Data Appl. **23**, 26 (2014)

19. Tian, D., et al.: An intrusion detection system based on machine learning for CAN-bus. In: Chen, Y., Duong, T.Q. (eds.) INISCOM 2017. LNICST, vol. 221, pp. 285–294. Springer, Cham (2018). https://doi.org/10.1007/978-3-319-74176-5_25

20. Zhu, K., Chen, Z., Peng, Y., Zhang, L.: Mobile edge assisted literal multidimensional anomaly detection of in-vehicle network using LSTM. IEEE Trans. Veh. Technol. **68**(5), 4275–4284 (2019)

Detection Algorithm Based on Eigenvalues of Sampling Covariance Matrix for Satellite Cognitive Network

Wenjie Zhou[✉], Dezhi Li, Zhenyong Wang, and Qing Guo

School of Electronics and Information Engineering, Harbin Institute of Technology, Harbin, China
22b305003@stu.hit.edu.cn, {lidezhi,ZYWang,qguo}@hit.edu.cn

Abstract. Satellite cognitive network is currently facing a lot of complex spectrum environment with a lot of interference, and the required user signal strength will change with a variety of external factors, which directly affects the above series of results obtained through the decision mechanism and it can not be well applied to satellite cognitive network. So a new blind detection algorithm based on maximum and minimum eigenvalues of sampling covariance matrix is proposed. In this algorithm, the ratio of the difference and sum of the maximum and minimum eigenvalues of the sampling covariance matrix is used as the perceptual decision quantity. Then, by introducing the latest results of the distribution of the maximum and minimum eigenvalues of the sampling covariance matrix in large dimensional random matrix, an effective decision threshold calculation method is designed. Compared with the classical eigenvalue detection algorithm, the new algorithm has the advantage of accurate calculation of perceptual decision threshold, and can effectively improve the detection performance and the reliability of decision results.

Keywords: Satellite cognitive network · Spectrum sensing · Detection based on sampling covariance eigenvalues

1 Introduction

Satellite cognitive network [1] in today's society is an important part as a space of cognitive network, not only can share resources of rational utilization and efficient spatial spectrum, but also can improve the network intelligent level, so as to efficiently promote the spatial heterogeneous network integration. Satellite cognitive network is currently the hot areas of satellite communication technology research and direction. However, spectrum sensing technology [2] is the foundation of satellite cognitive network construction, and spectrum sensing technology also determines its development. Because the satellite communication system has the characteristics of wide frequency range, complex node type, large space propagation loss and dynamic spectrum environment change, the traditional

J. Zhao (Ed.): WiSATS 2023, LNICST 509, pp. 44–55, 2023.
https://doi.org/10.1007/978-3-031-34851-8_4

spectrum sensing technology based on the ground wireless network environment is faced with many problems when it is applied to the satellite cognitive wireless network.

Traditional main user signal detection algorithms include matched filtering algorithm [3] and energy detection algorithm [4]. Although matched filtering algorithm has the best detection performance, it requires to obtain the prior statistics of the main user and channel and has limited application scenarios. ED algorithm does not need the prior information of the main user and channel, so it is simple to implement and generally has good detection performance. However, the biggest problem of the algorithm [5] is the scattering loss caused by the light of the satellite in the CN environment, the shadowing and signal weakness [6] will make the signal power sent to the low orbit satellite by the user on the high orbit satellite continuously decrease, and the signal strength to be received will not be stable all the time. Therefore, a Detection Algorithm based on Sampling Covariance Matrix (DASCM) is designed. The change of the maximum and minimum eigenvalues of the sampling covariance matrix of the received signal can well reflect the change of the main user's signal energy and related characteristics. The algorithm takes the ratio of the difference and sum of the maximum and minimum eigenvalues of the sample covariance matrix as the perceptual decision quantity, and uses the latest results of the asymptotic distribution of eigenvalues in the large dimensional random matrix to design an effective decision threshold calculation method.

2   Mathematical Model and Cognitive Scenario

2.1   Cognitive Scenario

Geo satellite and Leo satellite is to use the consistent range of frequencies, when high-orbit satellites are working, in order to prevent certain interference from low-orbit satellites. At this time, the detection algorithm based on sampling covariance matrix is considered, which can detect the transmission frequency of low orbit satellite to the main user uplink on the ground, this detection algorithm can also be used to set up a sensing link between the high orbit satellite and the base station on the ground. When working in high orbit satellite uplink, based on the sampling covariance matrix of the detection algorithm can get high orbit satellite signals emitted by base stations on the ground, when this occurs, should stop take up Leo satellite uplink real-time communication, so as to maximum avoid Leo satellite in high orbit satellite communication series of interference.

The spectrum of high orbit satellite (GEO) network is the authorization network, while that of low orbit satellite (LEO) network is the cognitive network.

How to reasonably allocate the frequency band resources of high orbit satellite and low orbit satellite is always a key research problem As shown in the figure below, the two satellites are involved in roughly the same scope. The system model is shown in the figure below (Fig. 1):

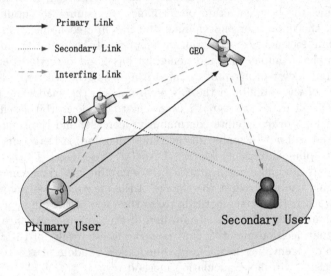

Fig. 1. GEO-LEO cognitive scenario.

2.2   Mathematical Model

Assume that the number of antennas required is M. Let the noise vector to be detected at n be $\mathbf{w}(n)$, the primary user vector $\mathbf{s}(n)$ and the acquired vector $\mathbf{x}(n)$ can be expressed as

$$\begin{cases} \mathbf{w}(n) = [w_1(n)w_2(n)\cdots w_M(n)]^{\mathrm{T}} \\ \mathbf{s}(n) = [s_1(n)s_2(n)\cdots s_M(n)]^{\mathrm{T}} \\ \mathbf{x}(n) = [x_1(n)x_2(n)\cdots x_M(n)]^{\mathrm{T}} \end{cases} \tag{1}$$

In the formula T is the transpose operation of the matrix. We assume that the main user signal and noise are independent of each other. According to the knowledge of signal detection theory, the following formula can be derived:

$$\begin{cases} H_0 : \mathbf{x}(n) = \mathbf{w}(n) \\ H_1 : \mathbf{x}(n) = \mathbf{s}(n) + \mathbf{w}(n) \end{cases} \tag{2}$$

Among them H_0 means the channel is not occupied at this time, when the channel is idle, only noise signals can be detected, H_1 means that the channel has both noise signals and master user signals, and the channel is occupied.$\mathbf{w}(n)$ is additive White Gaussian noise, its covariance matrix is $\sigma^2\mathbf{I}_M$. The above formula can be written in another way:

$$\begin{cases} H_0 : \mathbf{R}_x = E\left\{\mathbf{x}(n)\mathbf{x}^{\mathrm{T}}(n)\right\} = \sigma^2\mathbf{I}_M \\ H_1 : \mathbf{R}_x = E\left\{\mathbf{x}(n)\mathbf{x}^{\mathrm{T}}(n)\right\} = \mathbf{R}_s + \sigma^2\mathbf{I}_M \end{cases} \tag{3}$$

The covariance matrix of the received signals in the above equation are $\mathbf{R}_x$, $\mathbf{R}_s = E\left\{\mathbf{s}(n)\mathbf{s}^{\mathrm{T}}(n)\right\}$ is the covariance matrix of the master user signal. As can be seen from the above two formulas, assuming that the channel is occupied and idle, because of the generation of the master user signals, the covariance matrix of the received signals have different expressions. When we do this process, it is often difficult to get the covariance matrix information of the target signals. So in reality we replace the covariance matrix with the sample covariance matrix, it can be expressed as:

$$\hat{\mathbf{R}}_{x(n)} = \frac{1}{N}\sum_{i=1}^{N}\mathbf{x}(n)\mathbf{x}^{\mathrm{T}}(n) \tag{4}$$

When the number M of samples receiving signals in the sampling covariance matrix is larger, then it can be concluded that $\mathbf{R}_{x(n)} = \lim\limits_{N\to\infty}\hat{\mathbf{R}}_{x(n)}$. When the primary user signals do not exist, the sample covariance matrix of the received signals are consistent with that of the noise, that is

$$\hat{\mathbf{R}}_{w(n)} \stackrel{\Delta}{=} \hat{\mathbf{R}}_x \mid H_0 = \frac{1}{N}\sum_{n=1}^{N}\mathbf{w}(n)\mathbf{w}^{\mathrm{T}}(n) \tag{5}$$

3   Signal Detection Algorithm Based on Matrix Eigenvalue

3.1   Theoretical Analysis of DASCM Algorithm

We make the eigenvalue of the master user signals sampling covariance matrix are $\rho_i(i = 1, 2, \cdots M), \rho_1 \geq \rho_2 \geq \cdots \geq \rho_M$. It can be seen that when the channel is idle, the eigenvalues of the sampling covariance matrix of the received signals meet $\lambda_i = \sigma^2$, when the channel is occupied, eigenvalues meet $\lambda_i = \rho_i + \sigma^2(i = 1, \cdots, M)$. Therefore, it is easy to see that the generation of the main user signals will make the maximum eigenvalue and the minimum eigenvalue significantly different under the condition of channel idle and occupied. Let $\Delta = \lambda_1 - \lambda_2$ be the difference between them, when the channel is idle, $\lambda_1 \to \lambda_2$, we can draw $\Delta \to 0$. Again, when the channel is occupied, $\lambda_1 > \lambda_2$, we can draw $\Delta > 0$. As the power and relevance of the signals needed to be received increases, the fluctuation of the maximum and minimum eigenvalues increases when the channel is occupied and idle, therefore, we can further improve the detection algorithm according to this difference.

In addition, we found that if we only take Δ as the detection decision quantity we need, then, in the case of idle channel, the specific condition of detection decision depends on the quantity and integrity of noise. At the same time, it may cause the result to be excessively influenced by the prior information of noise variance. So, the performance of the detection algorithm constructed with Δ as the detection decision will still be disturbed by the uncertainty of noise, to prevent this, we need to make certain corrections:

$$T_{DASCM} = \frac{\Delta}{\lambda_1 + \lambda_2}$$
$$= \frac{\lambda_1 - \lambda_2}{\lambda_1 + \lambda_2} \tag{6}$$

e saw from the previous description that when the channel is idle, we can draw $T \to 0$, when the channel is occupied, we can draw $\Delta > 0$, $T > 0$. So, we can judge whether the channel is free by the state of T. In addition, when $\lambda_1 + \lambda_2$ detection result is idle, noise variance information is not needed to judge. On the other hand, the above formula can determine that T only depends on the received data, without relying on the prior information of the master users' signals. Therefore, we can obtain a completely blind detection algorithm according to the state of T.

3.2 Specific Flow of DASCM Algorithm

In general, the flow chart of sampling covariance matrix for decision taking T as a test decision quantity is shown below

---

Algorithm 1. DASCM master user signals detection flow chart

Calculate the sample covariance matrix
Calculate the maximum and minimum eigenvalues of the sampling covariance matrix
Calculate the detection decision T
Calculate the decision threshold φ according to P_f
if $T > \varphi$ then
   H_1
else
   H_0
end if

We start by taking signals from M antennas, So we get the M-dimensional vector of the received signals, and then we start counting the sample covariance matrix $\hat{\mathbf{R}}_{x(n)} = \frac{1}{N} \sum_{i=1}^{N} \mathbf{x}(n)\mathbf{x}^{\mathrm{T}}(n)$. The next step is to factor $\hat{\mathbf{R}}_x$ into the smallest and largest eigenvalues of λ_2 and λ_1, and then we can figure out $T_{DASCM} = \frac{\lambda_1 - \lambda_2}{\lambda_1 + \lambda_2}$. Then through the false alarm probability, the value of the threshold can be obtained, and finally the corresponding judgment results: when $T > \varphi$, the channel is occupied, when $T < \varphi$, the channel is free.

3.3 Calculation of Threshold of Decision Based on Sampling Covariance Matrix

One of the most important things when we do testing is how do we calculate the threshold φ. Through observation, it is found that there is a certain relationship between false alarm probability and judgment threshold:

$$
\begin{aligned}
P_{f\,DASCM} &= P(T > \varphi) \\
&= P(\frac{\lambda_1 - \lambda_M}{\lambda_1 + \lambda_M} > \varphi)
\end{aligned} \tag{7}
$$

Conversely, the above can also be expressed as:

$$
P_{f\,DASCM} = P\left(\frac{\frac{\lambda_1}{\lambda_2} - 1}{\frac{\lambda_1}{\lambda_2} + 1} > \varphi \right) \tag{8}
$$

It can be assumed that: $D = \frac{\lambda_1}{\lambda_2}$, substitute it into the above expression to obtain:

$$
\begin{aligned}
P_{f\,DASCM} &= P(\frac{D - 1}{D + 1} > \varphi) \\
&= P(D > \frac{1 + \varphi}{1 - \varphi})
\end{aligned} \tag{9}
$$

Suppose $d = \frac{1+\varphi}{1-\varphi}$, substitute in again to obtain:

$$
\begin{aligned}
P_{f\,DASCM} &= P(D > d) \\
&= P(\frac{\lambda_1}{\lambda_2} > d) \\
&= P(\lambda_1 > d\lambda_2)
\end{aligned} \tag{10}
$$

So in summary, if we set a certain false alarm probability in advance $P_{PRE} = P(T > \varphi)$, when the channel is idle, we can derive d from the probability density function of D, and then from the expression above for d and φ, finally, we can get the value of the threshold. Therefore, the most critical problem is the probability density function of D in the idle state of the channel. Some random matrix theory related knowledge is given below:

A: Assuming that $\lim\limits_{M,N \to \infty} \frac{M}{N} \to k$ $(0 < k < 1)$, then the maximum and minimum eigenvalues λ_2 and λ_1 of the sampling covariance matrix $\hat{\mathbf{R}}_{w(n)}$ of noise converge respectively to $\frac{\sigma^2}{N}(\sqrt{N} + \sqrt{M})^2$ and $\frac{\sigma^2}{N}(\sqrt{N} - \sqrt{M})^2$.

B: Assuming that $\lim\limits_{M,N\to\infty} \frac{M}{N} \to k$ $(0 < k < 1)$, set $\mu_1 = (\sqrt{N-1}+\sqrt{M})^2$, $v_1 = (\sqrt{N-1}+\sqrt{M})\left(\frac{1}{\sqrt{N-1}}+\frac{1}{\sqrt{M}}\right)^{1/3}$, $X = \frac{N\hat{R}_w}{\sigma^2}$. if $\lambda_1(X)$ is the largest eigenvalue of X, so $\frac{\lambda_1(X)-\mu_1}{v_1}$ obeys a first order TW distribution.

C: Assuming that $\lim\limits_{M,N\to\infty} \frac{M}{N} \to k$ $(0 < k < 1)$, set $\mu_2 = (\sqrt{N}-\sqrt{M})^2$, $v_2 = -(\sqrt{N}-\sqrt{M})\left(\frac{1}{\sqrt{M}}-\frac{1}{\sqrt{N}}\right)^{1/3}$, $X = \frac{N\hat{R}_w}{\sigma^2}$, if $\lambda_2(X)$ is the minimum eigenvalue of X, so $\frac{\lambda_2(X)-\mu_2}{v_2}$ obeys a first order TW distribution.

The distribution function of TW(Tracy-widow) can be defined as:

$$F_{DASCM}(t) = \exp\left(-\frac{1}{2}\int_t^\infty (q(u) + (u-t)q^2(u))\,du\right) \tag{11}$$

The $q(u)$ that appears in the formula above, we have the following equation:

$$q''(u)_{DASCM} = uq(u) + 2q^3(u) \tag{12}$$

According to the above conclusions, when the channel is idle, the limits of λ_1 and λ_2 obtained by sample covariance matrix can be expressed as follows:

$$\begin{aligned} \lambda_2 &\to \frac{\sigma^2}{N}(\sqrt{N}-\sqrt{M})^2 \\ \lambda_1 &\to \frac{\sigma^2}{N}(\sqrt{N}+\sqrt{M})^2 \end{aligned} \tag{13}$$

$$\begin{aligned} \lambda_1(X) &= \frac{N}{\sigma^2}\lambda_1 \\ \lambda_2(X) &= \frac{N}{\sigma^2}\lambda_2 \end{aligned} \tag{14}$$

Combined with the above results, the false alarm probability of λ_2 can be obtained as follows:

$$\begin{aligned} P_{fDASCM} &= P(\lambda_1 > d_0\lambda_2) \\ &= P(\lambda_1 > d_0\frac{\sigma^2}{N}(\sqrt{N}-\sqrt{M})^2) \\ &= P(\frac{N}{\sigma^2}\lambda_1 > d_0(\sqrt{N}-\sqrt{M})^2) \\ &= P(\lambda_1(\hat{A}) > d_0(\sqrt{N}-\sqrt{M})^2) \\ &= 1 - F_1(\frac{d_0(\sqrt{N}-\sqrt{M})^2) - \mu_1}{v_1}) \end{aligned} \tag{15}$$

From the expression of $F(.)$, it can be obtained:

$$d_0 = \frac{v_1 F_1^{-1}(1 - P_f) + \mu_1}{(\sqrt{N}-\sqrt{M})^2} \tag{16}$$

where $F_1^{-1}(.)$ is the inverse of $F_1(.)$.

Similarly, the false alarm probability of λ_1 is:

$$P_{fDASCM} \approx P(\lambda_1 > d_1 \frac{\sigma^2}{N} \lambda_2(X)) \tag{17}$$

We can also conclude that

$$d_1 = \frac{\left(\sqrt{N} + \sqrt{M}\right)^2}{v_2 F_1^{-1}(P_f) + \mu_2} \tag{18}$$

We take the average value of the two threshold values obtained above, and finally obtain a more accurate discriminant threshold value, that is:

$$d_{DASCM} = \frac{1}{2}\left[\frac{v_1 F_1^{-1}(1 - P_f) + \mu_1}{\left(\sqrt{N} - \sqrt{M}\right)^2} + \frac{\left(\sqrt{N} - \sqrt{M}\right)^2}{v_2 F_1^{-1}(1 - P_f) + \mu_2}\right] \tag{19}$$

We had $d = \frac{1+\varphi}{1-\varphi}$ before, and if we substitute that in, we can get:

$$\varphi_{DASCM} = 1 - \frac{4}{\left[\frac{v_1 F_1^{-1}(1-P_f)+\mu_1}{\left(\sqrt{N}-\sqrt{M}\right)^2} + \frac{\left(\sqrt{N}+\sqrt{M}\right)^2}{v_2 F_1^{-1}(P_f)+\mu_2}\right] + 2} \tag{20}$$

According to the derivation, when the master user signals are not accurately understood, the detection decision quantity of the sampling covariance matrix can be obtained, and then a relatively accurate decision threshold can be obtained to judge the existence of PU signal. So this algorithm can be widely used.

4   The Simulation Analysis

Our goal is to demonstrate the advantages of detection algorithms based on the ratio of the difference between the maximum and minimum eigenvalues of the sample covariance matrix, the traditional detection algorithm should be added in the simulation comparison. We assume that the preset false alarm probability value is $P_{FA} = 0.1$. The value of N is 200, the number of antennas M required is 8, after 5000 Monte Carlo simulations, the changes of P_d and P_f along with SNR of the two algorithms mentioned above are shown in the figure below, In the simulation figure, DASCM represents the simulation result of the improved algorithm, while PRE DASCM represents the simulation result of the previous classical and traditional detection algorithm (Fig. 2).

As can be seen from the above simulation results, there is a positive correlation between P_d and SNR of the two detection algorithms, P_d increases as SNR increases, when the SNR growth reaches a certain value, the detection

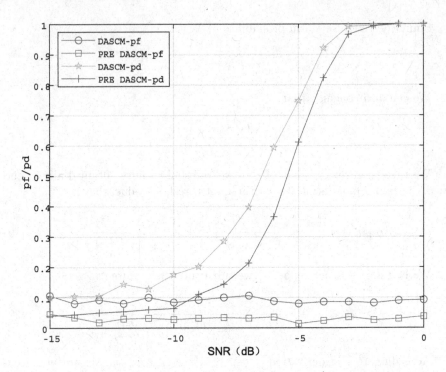

Fig. 2. P_d and P_f at different SNR ($N = 200$, $M = 8$).

algorithm can obtain 100 detection probability. However, the detection probability of DASCM can reach 100% earlier than that of PRE DASCM, this fully shows that the detection performance of DASCM algorithm studied above is better than that of PRE DASCM. Secondly, P_f of DASCM detection algorithm is closer to the pre-set false alarm probability value numerically than P_f of PRE DASCM detection algorithm. From this perspective, it can be seen that DASCM detection algorithm can obtain more accurate judgment threshold value compared with traditional detection algorithm, which also proves that the calculation method of judgment threshold studied in this section is accurate, and further reflects the superiority of DASCM detection algorithm.

We further want to explore the impact on the detection performance of this algorithm, We assume that the preset false alarm probability value is $P_{FA} = 0.1$. The value of N is 800, the number of antennas M required is 8, after 5000 Monte Carlo simulations, the simulation results that can be obtained are shown below. By comparing the obtained simulation graph with the above one, we can find that when the number of samples increases, the detection probability of these two detection algorithms also keeps increasing, forming a positive correlation trend. It can also be seen that the detection performance of DASCM detection algorithm is still better than that of traditional DASCM detection algorithm (Fig. 3).

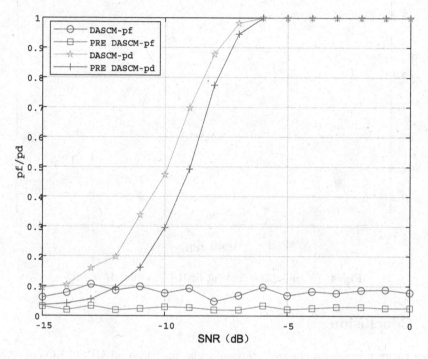

Fig. 3. P_d and P_f at different SNR ($N = 800$, $M = 8$).

Next, we want to explore what kind of interference the number of antennas M will bring to the detection performance of this algorithm. We assume that the preset false alarm probability value is $P_{FA} = 0.1$. The value of N is 200, the number of antennas M required is 10, after 5000 Monte Carlo simulations, the simulation results that can be obtained are shown below. By comparing the obtained simulation diagram with the one above, we can find that, when the number of antennas keeps increasing, the detection probability of these two detection algorithms also keeps increasing, forming a positive correlation trend, however, the effect of the new DASCM algorithm is better than that of the traditional algorithm even when the SNR values are different. The false alarm probability of the new DASCM algorithm is still approximately equal to 0.1, while the traditional detection method is far less than 0.1. Therefore, it is clear that the new DASCM algorithm is better for performance improvement (Fig. 4).

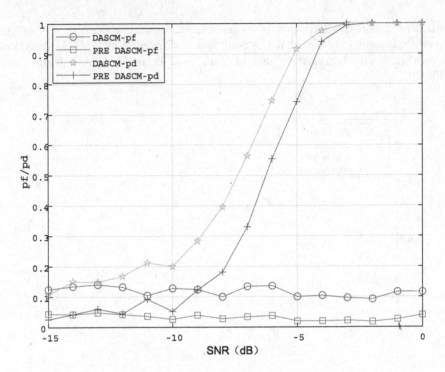

Fig. 4. P_d and P_f at different SNR ($N = 200$, $M = 10$).

5   Conclusion

This paper proposes a channel state information based on GEO-LEO cognitive scenarios. The current spectrum state can be sensed by building a channel state sensing model. Adopting a through the sampling covariance matrix of maximum and minimum eigenvalue of the numerical relationship of detection algorithm (DASCM), it is not need to know the PU signal of a priori knowledge, is a kind of blind detection, don't need to know the condition of second order moment of signal information, and can be a very accurate decision is obtained by calculating the threshold, the performance of the algorithm is greatly improved.

References

1. Cognitive Radio Technology. Academic Press (2009)
2. Guo, C., Guo, T., et al.: Investigation on key techniques and applications of cognitive radio. http://www.paper.edu.cn
3. Li, F., Li, Z.Q., Li, G.X., et al.: Efficient wideband spectrum sensing with maximal spectral efficiency for LEO mobile satellite systems. Sensors **17**(1), 193–217 (2017)
4. Mahal, J.A., Khawar, A., Abdelhadi, A., et al.: Spectral coexistence of MIMO radar and MIMO cellular system. IEEE Trans. Aerosp. Electron. Syst. AES **53**(2), 655–668 (2017)

5. Tarchi, D., Guidottti, A., Icolari, V., et al.: Technical challenges for cognitive radio application in satellite communications. In: IEEE CROWNCOM 2014. IEEE (2014)
6. Ren, G., Maroulas, V., Schizas, I.D.: Exploiting sensor mobility and covariance sparsity for distributed tracking of multiple sparse targets. EuraSIP J. Adv. Sig. Process. **2016**(1), 53 (2016)

Advanced Technologies in Wireless Communication Systems

Hybrid Beamforming Design for Multi-User Multi-Stream Communications with Terahertz Massive MIMO

Ziwei Wan[1], Tong Qin[1], Zhen Gao[1(✉)], Chun Hu[1], Yuezu Lv[1], Tuan Li[1], Chunli Zhu[1], and Jiening Mao[2]

[1] School of Information and Electronics, Beijing Institute of Technology, Beijing 100081, People's Republic of China
{ziweiwan,qintong,gaozhen16,bit_hc,yzlv,tuanli,chunlizhu}@bit.edu.cn
[2] Zhongxing Telecommunication Equipment (ZTE) Corporation, Shenzhen, Guangdong 518000, People's Republic of China
mao.jiening@zte.com.cn

Abstract. The hybrid beamforming (HBF) design for terahertz (THz) massive multiple-input multiple-output (mMIMO) communications is an essential but challenging problem in future wireless communications. In this paper, we propose an efficient HBF design framework for downlink multi-user multi-stream transmission in broadband THz mMIMO systems. First, the analytic solutions for digital precoder are derived to minimize the sum-mean-square error between the transmitted and received symbols. Then, we propose a tractable criterion for the codebook-based fully-connected analog precoder design, and further extend it to the case where the dynamic partially-connected structure is considered. A low-complexity energy-based greedy antenna grouping scheme is proposed for the dynamic hybrid structure. Simulation results demonstrate the effectiveness and the superiority of the proposed scheme in terms of sum rate and bit error rate over its counterparts.

Keywords: Terahertz (THz) · Hybrid beamforming (HBF) · Massive MIMO · Multi-user MIMO

1 Introduction

Given the spectrum crunch caused by ever-increasing connected devices and applications, terahertz (THz) technique is considered as a promising candidate for promoting future wireless communications [1]. Particularly, the cooperation between THz techniques and the state-of-the-art massive multiple-input multiple-output (mMIMO) system has received tremendous interest [1,2]. Equipped with a large number of antennas, mMIMO is able to compensate the severe path loss in the THz band and achieve finer-grain spatial multiplexing. However, it is impractical to deploy the power-aggressive fully-digital THz mMIMO, where one radio frequency chain (RFC) is dedicated for each

© ICST Institute for Computer Sciences, Social Informatics and Telecommunications Engineering 2023
Published by Springer Nature Switzerland AG 2023. All Rights Reserved
J. Zhao (Ed.): WiSATS 2023, LNICST 509, pp. 59–73, 2023.
https://doi.org/10.1007/978-3-031-34851-8_5

antenna. As a remedy, hybrid beamforming (HBF) architecture, which was initially applied to millimeter-wave (mmWave) mMIMO communications [3,4], has been considered for realizing THz mMIMO [5–7]. Similarly to the mmWave cases, it has been reported that the HBF architecture only requires much less RFCs to drive the entire antenna array to strike a balance between the hardware complexity, the power consumption, and the system performance.

Some preliminary THz HBF schemes have been proposed recently [5–7]. In [5], the HBF for THz non-orthogonal multiple access (NOMA) systems was investigated. The inversion of channel matrix with phase quantization was adopted as the analog precoder, while the low-complexity zero-forcing precoding was conducted for the digital counterpart. The authors of [6] proposed a two-stage hybrid beamforming scheme for THz mMIMO systems, which consists of a codebook searching algorithm and a regularized channel inversion method for analog and digital precoding, respectively. However, the prior works [5,6] did not consider the energy-efficient dynamic partially-connected structure in THz hybrid mMIMO, where the antennas are divided into several non-overlapped groups and the connection scheme between the antennas groups and the RFCs can be adjusted based on the real-time channel state information (CSI). A dynamic array-of-subarrays structure and the corresponding HBF design were proposed [7] for THz mMIMO, while the work [7] did not consider multi-user communications, which is vital in future THz cellular systems. The HBF design for multi-user multi-stream communications with THz mMIMO has not been well addressed at this stage.

In this paper, we propose a HBF design for multi-user multi-stream communications with THz mMIMO. The dynamic partially-connected structure is also considered to realize more resilient THz communications. Compared with the prior works [5–7], we consider a more generic communication scenario, namely multi-user multi-stream communications. We derive the analytic solutions for the digital precoder design to minimizes the sum-mean-square error (SMSE) between the transmitted and received symbols. As for the analog precoding in the dynamic partially-connected structure, a low-complexity codebook-based scheme is proposed based on a tractable criterion. Simulations are also conducted to verify the performance of the proposed scheme.

Notations: Lower-case and upper-case boldface letters denote vectors and matrices, respectively. $(\cdot)^T$, $(\cdot)^H$, and $\mathrm{tr}\,(\cdot)$ denote the transpose, conjugate transpose, and trace of an input matrix, respectively. $(\cdot)^{(i)}$ and $(\cdot)_{i,j}$ represent the i-th column vector and the i-th row and j-th column element of an input matrix, respectively. $\mathbf{I}_N$ denotes an $N \times N$ identity matrix, while $\mathbf{0}_{M \times N}$ denotes an all-zero matrix of size $M \times N$. Re(a) is the real part of a. $\|\cdot\|_2$, $\|\cdot\|_F$, diag $(\cdot)$, and $\mathbb{E}\,\{\cdot\}$ represent the ℓ_2-norm, Frobenius norm, (block) diagonalization, and statistical expectation, respectively. For a set $\mathcal{I}$, $|\mathcal{I}|_c$ is its cardinality, and setdiff $(\mathcal{I}, \{i\})$ denotes the operation that removes the element i from $\mathcal{I}$.

2   System Model

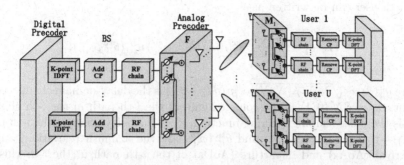

Fig. 1. The considered THz mMIMO system with HBF architecture. The BS supports multiple users with multi-stream transmission for each user.

We consider a multi-user THz mMIMO system with hybrid architecture at both the base station (BS) and users, as shown in Fig. 1. The BS employs N_t antennas and $M_t \ll N_t$ RFCs to simultaneously serve U users, and each user employs N_r antennas and $M_r \ll N_r$ RFCs to support $N_s \leq M_r$ data streams. Without loss of generality, we assume $N_s = M_r$ and $M_t = UM_r$. The analog part of the hybrid architecture consists of phase shifters and its specific structure will be discussed in the sequel. The orthogonal frequency division multiplexing (OFDM) with K sub-carriers and sampling period T_s is adopted in the system.

We denote the transmitted data symbols for the u-th ($1 \leq u \leq U$) user at the k-th ($1 \leq k \leq K$) sub-carrier as $\mathbf{x}_u[k] \in \mathbb{C}^{N_s \times 1}$. All the U users' data symbols are then concatenated as $\mathbf{x}[k] = \left[\mathbf{x}_1^H[k], ..., \mathbf{x}_U^H[k]\right]^H \in \mathbb{C}^{UN_s \times 1}$. We assume $\mathbb{E}\left\{\mathbf{x}[k]\mathbf{x}^H[k]\right\} = \mathbf{I}_{UN_s}$. Vector $\mathbf{x}[k]$ is precoded by the digital precoder $\mathbf{W}[k] = [\mathbf{W}_1[k], ..., \mathbf{W}_U[k]] \in \mathbb{C}^{M_t \times UN_s}$, where $\mathbf{W}_u[k] \in \mathbb{C}^{M_t \times N_s}$ is the dedicated digital precoders for the u-th user. After K-point inverse discrete Fourier transformation (DFT) and adding a cyclic prefix (CP), the BS forms the transmitted signals by using a frequency-flat analog precoder $\mathbf{F} \in \mathbb{C}^{N_t \times M_t}$. At the u-th user, the received signals are first combined with the frequency-flat analog combiner $\mathbf{M}_u \in \mathbb{C}^{N_r \times M_r}$. Then, after the removal of the CP and performing DFT, the digital combiner $\mathbf{V}_u[k] \in \mathbb{C}^{M_r \times N_s}$ is adopted to combine the received signals at the k-th sub-carrier. Therefore, in the downlink transmission, the received symbols at the k-th sub-carrier of the u-th user can be modeled as

$$\hat{\mathbf{x}}_u[k] = \mathbf{V}_u^H[k]\mathbf{M}_u^H\left(\mathbf{H}_u[k]\mathbf{F}\mathbf{W}[k]\mathbf{x}[k] + \mathbf{n}_u[k]\right), \tag{1}$$

where $\mathbf{H}_u[k] \in \mathbb{C}^{N_r \times N_t}$ is the effective frequency-domain channel at the k-th sub-carrier between the BS and u-th user. $\mathbf{n}_u[k] \in \mathbb{C}^{N_r \times 1}$ is the additive white Gaussian noise (AWGN) vector at the u-th user with zero mean and power σ^2.

The THz mMIMO channel is modeled as a sum of the contributions of N_c scattering clusters [1,7] and each cluster contains N_p propagation paths. Therefore, the channel impulse response (CIR) of THz mMIMO between the BS and the u-th user can be written as

$$\overline{\mathbf{H}}_u[d] = \sum_{i=1}^{N_c} \sum_{l=1}^{N_p} g_{il}^u(d) \mathbf{a}_r \left(\theta_{il}^{ru}, \phi_{il}^{ru}\right) \mathbf{a}_t^H \left(\theta_{il}^{tu}, \phi_{il}^{tu}\right), \tag{2}$$

where $g_{il}^u(d) = \sqrt{N_t N_r / (N_c N_p)} \alpha_{il}^u p \left(dT_s - \tau_{il}^u\right)$ is the delay-domain channel coefficient, $\alpha_{il}^u \sim \mathcal{CN}(0,1)$ is the complex gain of the i-th path in the l-th cluster, $p(\cdot)$ is the pulse shaping filtering function, τ_{il} is the delay-offset of the i-th path in the l-th cluster, $\theta_{il}^{ru} (\phi_{il}^{ru})$ and $\theta_{il}^{tu} (\phi_{il}^{tu})$ are the azimuth (elevation) angles of arrival (AoAs) and departure (AoDs) of the i-th path in the l-th cluster, respectively, and $\mathbf{a}_r (\theta_{il}^{ru}, \phi_{il}^{ru}) \in \mathbb{C}^{N_r \times 1}$ and $\mathbf{a}_t (\theta_{il}^{tu}, \phi_{il}^{tu}) \in \mathbb{C}^{N_t \times 1}$ are the normalized receive and transmit steering vectors, respectively. The superscript "u" in (2) corresponds to the u-th user. Throughout the paper, we assume that the half-wavelength spaced uniform planar array (UPA) is deployed at both the BS and users. Taking the BS as an example, the steering vector of the UPA with $N_t = N_y \times N_z$ elements can be written as

$$\mathbf{a}_t (\theta, \phi) = \frac{1}{\sqrt{N_y N_z}} \left[1, ..., e^{j\pi(n \sin\theta \cos\phi + m \sin\phi)}, \right.$$
$$\left. ..., e^{j\pi((N_y-1)\sin\theta \cos\phi + (N_z-1)\sin\phi)}\right]^T, \tag{3}$$

where $1 \leq n < N_y$ and $1 \leq m < N_z$. The receive steering vector $\mathbf{a}_r(\theta, \phi)$ can be similarly obtained. With the CIR in (2), the effective frequency-domain channel in (1) can be expressed as

$$\mathbf{H}_u[k] = \sum_{d=0}^{D-1} \overline{\mathbf{H}}_u[d] e^{-j\frac{2\pi k}{K}d}, \tag{4}$$

where $D > \max_{u,i,l} \{\tau_{il}^u\} / T_s$ is the length of the CP. Note that during the precoding design, the u-th user only knows its own CSI $\mathbf{H}_u[k]$, $\forall k$, while the global CSI $\mathbf{H}_u[k]$, $\forall u, k$, are available at the BS, which is a commonly adopted assumption in literature [4–8] for the investigation of the performance upper bound.

3   Problem Formulation

We propose to minimize the mean square error (MSE) between the transmitted and received symbols for the joint design of the analog and digital precoders. The u-th user's MSE at the k-th sub-carrier can be expressed as

$$\xi_u[k] = \mathbb{E}\left\{\left\|\beta^{-1}[k]\hat{\mathbf{x}}_u[k] - \mathbf{x}_u[k]\right\|_2^2\right\}, \tag{5}$$

where $\beta[k]$ is the normalization factor for the digital precoder $\mathbf{W}[k]$. By substituting (1) into (5), $\xi_u[k]$ can be further expressed as

$$
\begin{aligned}
\xi_u[k] =& \operatorname{tr}\left(\mathbf{V}_u^H[k]\,\mathbf{H}_{\text{eff}}^u[k]\,\tilde{\mathbf{W}}[k]\,\tilde{\mathbf{W}}^H[k]\,(\mathbf{H}_{\text{eff}}^u[k])^H\mathbf{V}_u[k]\right) \\
&- \operatorname{tr}\left(\tilde{\mathbf{W}}_u^H[k]\,(\mathbf{H}_{\text{eff}}^u[k])^H\mathbf{V}_u[k]\right) - \operatorname{tr}\left(\mathbf{V}_u^H[k]\,\mathbf{H}_{\text{eff}}^u[k]\,\tilde{\mathbf{W}}_u[k]\right) \\
&+ \sigma^2\beta^{-2}[k]\operatorname{tr}\left(\mathbf{V}_u^H[k]\,\mathbf{M}_u^H\mathbf{M}_u\mathbf{V}_u[k]\right) + N_s,
\end{aligned}
\tag{6}
$$

where $\mathbf{H}_{\text{eff}}^u[k] \triangleq \mathbf{M}_u^H\mathbf{H}_u[k]\mathbf{F} \in \mathbb{C}^{M_r \times M_t}$ represents the effective baseband channel, $\tilde{\mathbf{W}}[k] = \beta^{-1}[k]\mathbf{W}[k]$ is an effective digital precoder, and $\tilde{\mathbf{W}}_u[k] = \beta^{-1}[k]\mathbf{W}_u[k]$. Note that we leverage the independence among the transmitted symbols $\mathbf{x}[k]$ and the AWGN vector $\mathbf{n}_u[k]$ for obtaining (6). We assume that the analog part at the user is of fully-connected structure, while that at the BS is of dynamic partially-connected structure. The HBF design can be formulated as the following optimization problem:

$$
\underset{\{\mathbf{W}[k]\}_{k=1}^K,\{\mathbf{V}[k]\}_{k=1}^K,\mathbf{F},\mathbf{M}}{\text{minimize}} \sum_{k=1}^K \sum_{u=1}^U \xi_u[k]
\tag{7a}
$$

$$
\text{s.t.} \sum_{k=1}^K \operatorname{tr}\left(\mathbf{FW}[k]\mathbf{W}^H[k]\mathbf{F}^H\right) = P,
\tag{7b}
$$

$$
|\mathbf{F}_{i,j}| \in \{0, \frac{1}{\sqrt{N_t}}\}, \left|(\mathbf{M}_u)_{i,j}\right| = \frac{1}{\sqrt{N_r}}, \forall i,j,u,
\tag{7c}
$$

where $\mathbf{V}[k] = \operatorname{diag}(\mathbf{V}_1[k],...,\mathbf{V}_U[k])$, $\mathbf{M} = \operatorname{diag}(\mathbf{M}_1,...,\mathbf{M}_U)$, and P is the total transmit power. Note that $|\mathbf{F}_{i,j}| = 0$ means that there is no connection between the i-th RF chain and the j-th transmit antenna.

4 Proposed Hybrid Beamforming Scheme

In this section, we first derive the digital precoding solution based on the min-SMSE criterion. Then, we further propose a codebook-based scheme for analog precoding design under dynamic partially-connected structure.

4.1 Digital Precoding Design

We first focus on the digital precoder/combiner design while fixing the analog precoder/combiner. Based on (7), the digital precoder/combiner design problem can be rewritten as

$$
\underset{\{\mathbf{W}[k]\}_{k=1}^K,\{\mathbf{V}[k]\}_{k=1}^K}{\text{minimize}} \sum_{k=1}^K \sum_{u=1}^U \xi_u[k]
\tag{8a}
$$

$$
\text{s.t.} \sum_{k=1}^K \operatorname{tr}\left(\mathbf{FW}[k]\mathbf{W}^H[k]\mathbf{F}^H\right) = P.
\tag{8b}
$$

Given the limited CSI at the user side and the independence among the sub-carriers, we decompose the problem (8) into the subproblems that minimizing $\xi_u[k]$ for each u and k when designing the digital combiners. For the unconstrained $\mathbf{V}_u^H[k]$, we let the partial derivative $\frac{\partial \xi_u[k]}{\partial \mathbf{V}_u^H[k]}$ ($\xi_u[k]$ is shown in (6)) equal to zero and thus obtain

$$\mathbf{V}_u^H[k] = \tilde{\mathbf{W}}_u^H[k]\left(\mathbf{H}_{\text{eff}}^u[k]\right)^H \mathbf{A}^{-1}, \tag{9}$$

where

$$\mathbf{A} \triangleq \mathbf{H}_{\text{eff}}^u[k]\tilde{\mathbf{W}}[k]\tilde{\mathbf{W}}^H[k]\left(\mathbf{H}_{\text{eff}}^u[k]\right)^H + \sigma^2\beta^{-2}[k]\mathbf{M}_u^H\mathbf{M}_u.$$

On the other hand, we design the digital precoder $\mathbf{W}[k]$ at the BS in order to minimize the SMSE of all users, namely $\xi[k] = \sum_{u=1}^U \xi_u[k]$, which can be written as

$$\begin{aligned}\xi[k] =& \beta^{-2}[k]\operatorname{tr}(\mathbf{B}) - \beta^{-1}[k]\operatorname{tr}\left(\mathbf{W}^H[k]\mathbf{H}_{\text{eff}}^H[k]\mathbf{V}[k]\right)\\&- \beta^{-1}[k]\operatorname{tr}\left(\mathbf{V}^H[k]\mathbf{H}_{\text{eff}}[k]\mathbf{W}[k]\right)\\&+ \sigma^2\beta^{-2}[k]\operatorname{tr}\left(\mathbf{V}^H[k]\mathbf{M}^H\mathbf{M}\mathbf{V}[k]\right) + UN_s,\end{aligned} \tag{10}$$

where $\mathbf{B} \triangleq \mathbf{V}^H[k]\mathbf{H}_{\text{eff}}[k]\mathbf{W}[k]\mathbf{W}^H[k]\mathbf{H}_{\text{eff}}^H[k]\mathbf{V}[k]$ and $\mathbf{H}_{\text{eff}}[k] = \left[\left(\mathbf{H}_{\text{eff}}^1[k]\right)^H, \ ..., \left(\mathbf{H}_{\text{eff}}^U[k]\right)^H\right]^H \in \mathbb{C}^{UM_r \times M_t}$. To seek the optimal digital precoder with the transmit power constraint, we introduce a Lagrangian multiplier $\mu[k]$ and construct the Lagrangian function as

$$L = \xi[k] + \mu[k]\left(\operatorname{tr}\left(\mathbf{F}\mathbf{W}[k]\mathbf{W}^H[k]\mathbf{F}^H\right) - \tilde{P}\right), \tag{11}$$

where $\tilde{P} = P/K$ denotes the transmit power for each sub-carrier after uniform power allocation among sub-carrier. Letting the partial derivative $\frac{\partial L}{\partial \mathbf{W}[k]}$ equal to zero yields

$$\mathbf{W}[k] = \beta[k]\mathbf{C}^{-1}\mathbf{H}_{\text{eff}}^H[k]\mathbf{V}[k], \tag{12}$$

where $\mathbf{C} \triangleq \mathbf{H}_{\text{eff}}^H[k]\mathbf{V}[k]\mathbf{V}^H[k]\mathbf{H}_{\text{eff}}[k] + \mu[k]\beta^2[k]\mathbf{F}^H\mathbf{F}$. Similarly, let the partial derivative $\frac{\partial L}{\partial \beta[k]}$ equal to zero and we arrive at

$$\begin{aligned}\beta[k]\operatorname{Re}\left\{\operatorname{tr}\left(\mathbf{V}^H[k]\mathbf{H}_{\text{eff}}[k]\mathbf{W}[k]\right)\right\}\\- \operatorname{tr}(\mathbf{B}) - \sigma^2\operatorname{tr}\left(\mathbf{V}^H[k]\mathbf{M}^H\mathbf{M}\mathbf{V}[k]\right) = 0.\end{aligned} \tag{13}$$

We introduce the following Lemma 1 to further simplify (13).

Lemma 1. *Our proposed precoding design in the sequel will render*

$$\operatorname{Re}\left\{\operatorname{tr}\left(\mathbf{V}^H[k]\mathbf{H}_{\text{eff}}[k]\tilde{\mathbf{W}}[k]\right)\right\} = \operatorname{tr}\left(\mathbf{V}^H[k]\mathbf{H}_{\text{eff}}[k]\tilde{\mathbf{W}}[k]\right), \tag{14}$$

i.e., all the diagonal elements of $\mathbf{V}^H[k]\mathbf{H}_{\text{eff}}[k]\tilde{\mathbf{W}}[k]$ are real numbers.

Proof. Note that

$$\mathrm{tr}\left(\mathbf{V}^H\left[k\right]\mathbf{H}_{\mathrm{eff}}\left[k\right]\tilde{\mathbf{W}}\left[k\right]\right) = \sum_{u=1}^{U}\mathrm{tr}\left(\mathbf{V}_u^H\left[k\right]\mathbf{H}_{\mathrm{eff}}^u\left[k\right]\tilde{\mathbf{W}}_u\left[k\right]\right), \qquad (15)$$

and thus **Lemma** 1 can be proven by noticing from (27) that $\mathbf{V}_u^H\left[k\right]\mathbf{H}_{\mathrm{eff}}^u\left[k\right]\tilde{\mathbf{W}}_u\left[k\right]$, $\forall u$, are positive semi-definite matrices, whose diagonal elements are obviously real numbers. □

According to Lemma 1, we can safely remove the symbol $\mathrm{Re}\left\{\cdot\right\}$ in (13). Then, based on (13), we have

$$\mu\left[k\right]\beta^2\left[k\right] = \sigma^2\mathrm{tr}\left(\mathbf{V}^H\left[k\right]\mathbf{M}^H\mathbf{M}\mathbf{V}\left[k\right]\right)/\tilde{P}. \qquad (16)$$

Apparently, if we substitute (16) into (12), $\tilde{\mathbf{W}}\left[k\right]$ can be solved accordingly, even though the specific values of $\mu\left[k\right]$ and $\beta\left[k\right]$ are unknown. The actual digital precoder can be obtained as $\mathbf{W}\left[k\right] = \beta\left[k\right]\tilde{\mathbf{W}}\left[k\right]$ with

$$\beta\left[k\right] = \sqrt{\tilde{P}/\mathrm{tr}\left(\mathbf{F}\tilde{\mathbf{W}}\left[k\right]\tilde{\mathbf{W}}^H\left[k\right]\mathbf{F}^H\right)}. \qquad (17)$$

With the closed-form solutions (9) and (12), it is natural to conduct an alternating optimization, i.e., to optimize $\mathbf{W}\left[k\right]$ or $\mathbf{V}_u\left[k\right]$ by fixing another as constant and repeat until convergence, at the cost of prohibitive computational complexity. Fortunately, it has been verified in [9] that if an appropriate initial value $\mathbf{V}_{\mathrm{ini}}$ is chosen and assigned to $\mathbf{V}\left[k\right]$, a sufficiently good performance can be guaranteed even without the alternating optimization. Specifically, we set

$$\mathbf{V}_{\mathrm{ini}} = \mathrm{diag}\left(\mathbf{V}_{\mathrm{ini}}^1, ..., \mathbf{V}_{\mathrm{ini}}^U\right), \qquad (18)$$

where $\left\{\mathbf{V}_{\mathrm{ini}}^u\right\}_{u=1}^U$ are arbitrary unitary matrices. We propose the following procedure to design the digital precoder/combiner. Firstly, $\mathbf{V}_{\mathrm{ini}}$ in (18) is used as the initial solution of the digital combiners of all users and is substituted into (12) to obtain the digital precoder at the BS. Then, the obtained digital precoder is substituted into (9) to update the digital combiners at the users. It has been reported in [9] that the above procedure without alternating optimization guarantees $\mathbf{V}^H\left[k\right]\mathbf{H}_{\mathrm{eff}}\left[k\right]\tilde{\mathbf{W}}\left[k\right]$ to be a (nearly) diagonal matrix, eliminating the inter-user and inter-stream interferences. Interested readers are referred to [9] for more details.

4.2 Analog Precoding with Fully-Connected Structure

We first consider the analog precoding design for the fully-connected architecture at the BS with the obtained digital part, and the proposed scheme will be extended to the dynamic partially-connected architecture in the next subsection. The analog precoding design problem with the known digital precoder/combiner can be written as

$$\underset{\{\mathbf{M}_u\}_{u=1}^U, \mathbf{F}}{\text{minimize}} \sum_{k=1}^{K} \xi[k], \tag{19a}$$

$$\text{s.t. } \left|(\mathbf{M}_u)_{i,j}\right| = \frac{1}{\sqrt{N_r}}, |\mathbf{F}_{i,j}| = \frac{1}{\sqrt{N_t}}, \forall i, j, u. \tag{19b}$$

Based on (13) and (10), we can obtain that when the proposed digital pre-coder/combiner are applied, the following equation holds

$$\xi[k] = UN_s - \beta^{-1}[k] \operatorname{tr}\left(\mathbf{V}^H[k]\mathbf{H}_{\text{eff}}[k]\mathbf{W}[k]\right)$$
$$= UN_s - \operatorname{tr}\left(\mathbf{V}^H[k]\mathbf{H}_{\text{eff}}[k]\tilde{\mathbf{W}}[k]\right), \tag{20}$$

which indicates that we can improve $\xi[k]$ by maximizing $\operatorname{tr}\left(\mathbf{V}^H[k]\mathbf{H}_{\text{eff}}[k]\tilde{\mathbf{W}}[k]\right)$.

To further characterize the impact of $\mathbf{H}_{\text{eff}}$ on $\xi[k]$, in the rest of this section, we assume that $\mathbf{F}^H\mathbf{F} = \mathbf{I}_{M_t}$ and $\mathbf{M}^H\mathbf{M} = \mathbf{I}_{UM_r}$, which can be perfectly satisfied via the proposed codebook-based analog precoding design, as detailed hereinafter. Recall that $\{\mathbf{V}_{\text{ini}}^u\}_{u=1}^U$ are unitary matrices, so we have $\mu[k]\beta^2[k] = \sigma^2\operatorname{tr}\left(\mathbf{M}^H\mathbf{M}\right)/\tilde{P} \approx \sigma^2 UM_r/\tilde{P}$ based on (16). Therefore, according to (12), the obtained digital precoder (without power constraint) can be written as $\tilde{\mathbf{W}}[k] = \left(\mathbf{H}_{\text{eff}}^H[k]\mathbf{H}_{\text{eff}}[k] + \varepsilon\mathbf{I}_{M_t}\right)^{-1}\mathbf{H}_{\text{eff}}^H[k]\mathbf{V}_{\text{ini}}$, that is

$$\tilde{\mathbf{W}}_u[k] = \left(\mathbf{H}_{\text{eff}}^H[k]\mathbf{H}_{\text{eff}}[k] + \varepsilon\mathbf{I}_{M_t}\right)^{-1}(\mathbf{H}_{\text{eff}}^u[k])^H\mathbf{V}_{\text{ini}}^u, \tag{21}$$

where $\varepsilon \overset{\Delta}{=} \sigma^2 UM_r/\tilde{P}$ and $\mathbf{V}_{\text{ini}}$ is the initial value for the design of digital part, as shown in (18). Moreover, by substituting $\mathbf{M}^H\mathbf{M} \approx \mathbf{I}_{UM_r}$ into (9), we have

$$\mathbf{V}_u^H[k] \approx \tilde{\mathbf{W}}_u^H[k](\mathbf{H}_{\text{eff}}^u[k])^H$$
$$\left(\mathbf{H}_{\text{eff}}^u[k]\tilde{\mathbf{W}}[k]\tilde{\mathbf{W}}^H[k](\mathbf{H}_{\text{eff}}^u[k])^H + \sigma^2\beta^{-2}[k]\mathbf{I}_{M_r}\right)^{-1}. \tag{22}$$

To simplify the representation in (22), we consider the singular value decomposition (SVD) of $\mathbf{H}_{\text{eff}}[k]$, that is

$$\mathbf{H}_{\text{eff}}[k] = \mathbf{L}[k]\boldsymbol{\Sigma}[k]\mathbf{R}^H[k], \tag{23}$$

where $\mathbf{L}[k] \in \mathbb{C}^{UM_r \times UM_r}$ and $\mathbf{R}[k] \in \mathbb{C}^{M_t \times M_t}$ are unitary matrices, and $\boldsymbol{\Sigma}[k] = \operatorname{diag}(b_1[k], ..., b_{M_t}[k])$ is a diagonal matrix with the non-zero singular values $b_n[k]$, $1 \leq n \leq M_t$, on its diagonal, since we have assumed that $M_t = UM_r$ and the channel matrices are rank-sufficient for multi-stream communications. By denoting $\mathbf{L}[k] = \left[\mathbf{L}_1^H[k], ..., \mathbf{L}_U^H[k]\right]^H$ with each $\mathbf{L}_u[k] \in \mathbb{C}^{M_r \times UM_r}$, we obtain

$$\mathbf{H}_{\text{eff}}^u[k] = \mathbf{L}_u[k]\boldsymbol{\Sigma}[k]\mathbf{R}^H[k]. \tag{24}$$

By exploiting (23) and (24), we simplify (22) as

$$\mathbf{V}_u^H[k] = \mathbf{D}\left(\mathbf{D}^H\mathbf{D} + \sigma^2\beta^{-2}[k]\mathbf{I}_{M_r}\right)^{-1}, \tag{25}$$

where the auxiliary matrix $\mathbf{D}$ can be expressed as

$$\mathbf{D} = (\mathbf{V}_{\text{ini}}^u)^H \mathbf{S}_u [k] \left(\mathbf{I}_{UM_r} + \varepsilon \boldsymbol{\Sigma}^{-2} [k] \right)^{-1} \mathbf{S}_u^H [k] . \tag{26}$$

With (25)–(26), the effective channel for the u-th user $\mathbf{V}_u^H [k] \mathbf{H}_{\text{eff}}^u [k] \tilde{\mathbf{W}}_u [k]$ can be written as

$$\mathbf{V}_u^H [k] \mathbf{H}_{\text{eff}}^u [k] \tilde{\mathbf{W}}_u [k] = \mathbf{D} \left(\mathbf{D}^H \mathbf{D} + \sigma^2 \beta^{-2} [k] \mathbf{I}_{M_r} \right)^{-1} \mathbf{D}^H . \tag{27}$$

For ease of further analysis, we focus on a large signal-to-noise-ratio (SNR) limit such that $\varepsilon = \sigma^2 U M_r / \tilde{P} \to 0$. This assumption has been adopted in the previous work on mmWave HBF [9], and it is also reasonable in THz mMIMO communications, since higher antenna gain and array gain can be achieved by THz antenna elements [1] with the known CSI during precoding stage. In such cases, $\mathbf{D}$ in (26) approximates to $(\mathbf{V}_{\text{ini}}^u)^H$, and thus we have

$$\mathrm{tr} \left(\mathbf{V}_u^H [k] \mathbf{H}_{\text{eff}}^u [k] \tilde{\mathbf{W}}_u [k] \right) = \mathrm{tr} \left(\mathbf{D}^H \mathbf{D} (\mathbf{D}^H \mathbf{D} + \sigma^2 \beta^{-2} [k] \mathbf{I}_{M_r})^{-1} \right)$$
$$\overset{\varepsilon \to 0}{=} \frac{M_r}{1 + \sigma^2 \beta^{-2} [k]}, \tag{28}$$

where

$$\beta^2 [k] = \frac{\tilde{P}}{\mathrm{tr} \left((\boldsymbol{\Sigma}^2 [k] + \varepsilon \mathbf{I}_{M_t})^{-1} \boldsymbol{\Sigma}^2 [k] (\boldsymbol{\Sigma}^2 [k] + \varepsilon \mathbf{I}_{M_t})^{-1} \right)} \overset{\varepsilon \to 0}{=} \frac{\tilde{P}}{\sum\limits_{i=1}^{M_t} \frac{1}{b_i^2 [k]}}, \tag{29}$$

according to (17).

Substituting (27) and (29) into (20), we can rewrite $\xi [k]$ as

$$\xi [k] = U N_s - \sum_{u=1}^{U} \mathrm{tr} \left(\mathbf{V}_u^H [k] \mathbf{H}_{\text{eff}}^u [k] \tilde{\mathbf{W}}_u [k] \right) = \frac{U N_s \sigma^2}{\frac{\tilde{P}}{\sum\limits_{i=1}^{M_t} \frac{1}{b_i^2 [k]}} + \sigma^2} . \tag{30}$$

It is obvious that $\xi [k]$ decreases with $b_n^2 [k]$ increasing, $\forall n$, which sheds light on how to design the analog precoder/combiner to improve the SMSE. As a heuristic method, we can maximize $\sum\limits_{k=1}^{K} \sum\limits_{i=1}^{M_t} b_i^2 [k] = \mathrm{tr} \left(\mathbf{H}_{\text{eff}} [k] \mathbf{H}_{\text{eff}}^H [k] \right)$. Furthermore, given that $\mathbf{H}_{\text{eff}}$ should be a (nearly) diagonal matrix to eliminate interferences such that $\mathrm{tr} \left(\mathbf{H}_{\text{eff}} [k] \mathbf{H}_{\text{eff}}^H [k] \right) \approx \sum\limits_{i=1}^{M_t} \left| (\mathbf{H}_{\text{eff}} [k])_{i,i} \right|^2$, we can maximize the sum of the squares of the modulus of diagonal entries in $\mathbf{H}_{\text{eff}} [k]$, $\sum\limits_{i=1}^{M_t} \left| (\mathbf{H}_{\text{eff}} [k])_{i,i} \right|^2$. On the other hand, to realize low-complexity computations and affordable feedback overhead for THz communications, we consider that the analog precoders (i.e., $\mathbf{M}_u^{(m)}$ and $\mathbf{F}^{(m)}$) can only be constructed from the two-dimensional DFT codebooks $\mathcal{D}_{r,u}$ and $\mathcal{D}_t$, respectively. Using the obtained optimization objective (i.e., $\sum_{i=1}^{M_t} \left| (\mathbf{H}_{\text{eff}}[k])_{i,i} \right|^2$) and codebooks, the analog precoding problem turns into

$$\underset{\{\mathbf{M}_u\}_{u=1}^U, \mathbf{F}}{\text{maximize}} \sum_{k=1}^K \sum_{u=1}^U \sum_{m=1}^{N_s} \left| \left(\mathbf{M}_u^{(m)}\right)^H \mathbf{H}_u[k] \mathbf{F}_u^{(m)} \right|^2 \tag{31a}$$

$$\text{s.t.} \mathbf{M}_u^{(m)} \in \mathcal{D}_{r,u}, \mathbf{F}_u^{(m)} \in \mathcal{D}_t, \forall m, u, \tag{31b}$$

We propose an iterative greedy algorithm to solve (31), as described in **Algorithm 1**. Specifically, in each iteration, we select the optimal codeword-pair from the corresponding codebooks as the columns of analog precoder and combiner based on the criterion in (31). Note that we adopt (two-dimensional) DFT codewords in $\mathcal{D}_t$ and $\mathcal{D}_{t,u}$ so that the orthogonality assumptions $\mathbf{F}^H \mathbf{F} = \mathbf{I}_{M_t}$ and $\mathbf{M}^H \mathbf{M} = \mathbf{I}_{UM_r}$ in previous analysis can be perfectly satisfied.

Algorithm 1. Proposed Analog Precoding Design

Input: The codebooks $\mathcal{D}_t$ and $\mathcal{D}_{r,u}$, and $\mathbf{H}_u[k]$, $\forall u, k$.

1: Initialization: $\mathcal{U} = \{1, ..., U\}$, $\mathbf{F}_u = \mathbf{M}_u = $ empty matrix, $\forall u$;

2: **while** $|\mathcal{U}|_c > 0$ **do**

3:    $\{u^{\text{opt}}, \mathbf{a}_r^{\text{opt}}, \mathbf{a}_t^{\text{opt}}\} = \underset{u \in \mathcal{U}, \mathbf{a}_r \in \mathcal{D}_{r,u}, \mathbf{a}_t \in \mathcal{D}_t}{\arg\max} \sum_{k=1}^K \left\| \mathbf{a}_r^H \mathbf{H}_u[k] \mathbf{a}_t \right\|_2^2$;

4:    $\mathbf{M}_{u^{\text{opt}}} = [\mathbf{M}_{u^*} | \mathbf{a}_r^{\text{opt}}]$, $\mathbf{F}_{u^{\text{opt}}} = [\mathbf{F}_{u^{\text{opt}}} | \mathbf{a}_t^{\text{opt}}]$;

5:    $\mathcal{D}_{r,u^{\text{opt}}} = \text{setdiff}\left(\mathcal{D}_{r,u^{\text{opt}}}, \{\mathbf{a}_r^{\text{opt}}\}\right)$;

6:    $\mathcal{D}_t = \text{setdiff}\left(\mathcal{D}_t, \{\mathbf{a}_t^{\text{opt}}\}\right)$;

7:    **if** the column number of $\mathbf{M}_{u^{\text{opt}}}$ is M_r, **then**

8:       $\mathcal{U} = \text{setdiff}\left(\mathcal{U}, \{u^{\text{opt}}\}\right)$;

9:    **end if**

10: **end while**

Output: Analog precoders $\mathbf{F}_u$ and combiners $\mathbf{M}_u$, $\forall u$.

4.3 Analog Precoding with Dynamic Partially-Connected Structure

In this subsection, we further consider the analog precoding design when the BS adopts the dynamic partially-connected structure. As shown in Fig. 2, in the considered dynamic structure, both antennas and RFCs are divided into U non-overlapped groups. Each antenna group has N_t/U (which is assume to be an integer) antennas, while each RFC group has N_s RFCs. There is a one-to-one mapping between U antenna groups and U RFC groups, and the fully-connected architecture is applied within each group-pair. Note that the antenna indices in each antenna group can be dynamically adjusted based on CSI, which provides more DoFs for THz communications compared to the fixed partially-connected architecture [5,6]. Let $\mathcal{A}_n \subseteq \{1, ..., N_t\}$ denotes the antenna indices set of the

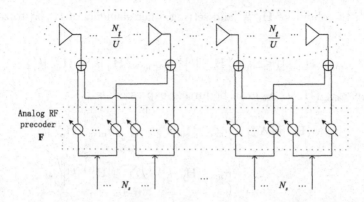

Fig. 2. A dynamic partially-connected hybrid architecture at the BS.

n-th antenna group, $1 \leq n \leq U$, with $|\mathcal{A}_u|_c = N_t/U$ and $\mathcal{A}_u \cap \mathcal{A}_{u'} = \emptyset$ for $u \neq u'$. Accordingly, the problem (31) can be re-formulated under the dynamic architecture as the following optimization problem

$$\underset{\{\mathcal{A}_n\}_{n=1}^{U},\{\mathbf{M}_u\}_{u=1}^{U},\mathbf{F}}{\text{maximize}} \sum_{u=1}^{U}\sum_{m=1}^{N_s}\sum_{k=1}^{K}\left|\left(\mathbf{M}_u^{(m)}\right)^H \mathbf{H}_u[k]\mathbf{\Lambda}_u\mathbf{F}_u^{(m)}\right|^2 \tag{32a}$$

$$\text{s.t.} \mathbf{M}_u^{(m)} \in \mathcal{D}_{r,u}, \mathbf{F}_u^{(m)} \in \mathcal{D}_t, \forall m, u, \tag{32b}$$

$$(\mathbf{\Lambda}_u)_{i,j} = \begin{cases} 1, & \text{if } i = j \text{ and } i \in \mathcal{A}_u \\ 0, & \text{Otherwise} \end{cases}. \tag{32c}$$

It is clear that once $\mathcal{A}_u$, or equivalently $\mathbf{\Lambda}_u$, $\forall u$, are determined, problem (32) will be the same as problem (31) by treating $\mathbf{H}_u[k]\mathbf{\Lambda}_u$, $\forall u$, as new effective channels. Inspired by this observation, we focus on the antenna grouping design. Basically, the antenna grouping problem is a combinatorial optimization problem and it requires extremely complicated exhaustive search to obtain the optimal solution. As a remedy, we propose a low-complexity alternative in the sequel. Note that

$$\left|\left(\mathbf{M}_u^{(m)}\right)^H \mathbf{H}_u[k]\mathbf{\Lambda}_u\mathbf{F}_u^{(m)}\right| \leq \sigma_{\max}(\mathbf{H}_u[k]\mathbf{\Lambda}_u). \tag{33}$$

holds for any normalized vectors $\mathbf{M}_u^{(m)}$ and $\mathbf{F}_u^{(m)}$, where $\sigma_{\max}(\mathbf{H}_u[k]\mathbf{\Lambda}_u)$ is the maximal singular value of $\mathbf{H}_u[k]\mathbf{\Lambda}_u$. (33) can be proven by considering the compatibility between the vector norm and the matrix norm [10]. For ease of analysis, we assume that $\mathbf{M}_u^{(m)}$ and $\mathbf{F}_u^{(m)}$ have been optimized when designing antenna grouping such that $\left|\left(\mathbf{M}_u^{(m)}\right)^H \mathbf{H}_u[k]\mathbf{\Lambda}_u\mathbf{F}_u^{(m)}\right| = \sigma_{\max}(\mathbf{H}_u[k]\mathbf{\Lambda}_u)$. In this way, we can focus only on how to design $\mathbf{\Lambda}_u$ to maximize $\sigma_{\max}(\mathbf{H}_u[k]\mathbf{\Lambda}_u)$. We introduce a notation $\mathbf{H}_u^{\langle i \rangle}[k]$ representing a matrix obtained by reserving only the i-th column of $\mathbf{H}_u[k]$ and setting other elements of $\mathbf{H}_u[k]$ to zero. We have [10]

$$\sigma_{\max}(\mathbf{H}_u[k]) \leq \sigma_{\max}\left(\mathbf{H}_u^{\langle i\rangle}[k]\right) + \sigma_{\max}\left(\mathbf{H}_u[k] - \mathbf{H}_u^{\langle i\rangle}[k]\right). \tag{34}$$

Therefore, $\sigma_{\max}(\mathbf{H}_u[k]\,\mathbf{\Lambda}_u)$ can be further expressed as

$$\sigma_{\max}(\mathbf{H}_u[k]\,\mathbf{\Lambda}_u) \overset{(a)}{\geq} \sigma_{\max}(\mathbf{H}_u[k]) - \sum_{i \notin \mathcal{A}_u} \sigma_{\max}\left(\mathbf{H}_u^{\langle i\rangle}[k]\right)$$

$$\overset{(b)}{=} \sigma_{\max}(\mathbf{H}_u[k]) - \sum_{i \notin \mathcal{A}_u} \left\|\mathbf{H}_u^{(i)}[k]\right\|_2, \tag{35}$$

where (a) is obtained by applying (34) for each $i \notin \mathcal{A}_u$, and (b) is because for the rank-1 matrix $\mathbf{H}_u^{\langle i\rangle}[k]$, its maximal singular value equals to its Frobenius norm, and futher equals to the ℓ_2-norm of its i-th column vector. It is observed from (35) that $\sigma_{\max}(\mathbf{H}_u[k]\,\mathbf{\Lambda}_u)$ increases as the sum ℓ_2-norm of the unselected columns in $\mathbf{H}_u[k]$ decreasing. In other words, given $\mathbf{H}_u[k]$, we can reserve the N_t/U columns with the most significant ℓ_2-norms and allocate the corresponding antennas to the u-th user to maximize $\sigma_{\max}(\mathbf{H}_u[k]\,\mathbf{\Lambda}_u)$, and further to reduce SMSE. Based on the analysis above, the proposed low-complexity energy-based greedy antenna grouping algorithm are summarized in Algorithm 2. Note that once the antenna grouping is completed, the analog precoding design in Algorithm 1 can be directly applied to solve (32).

Algorithm 2. Energy-based Greedy Antenna Grouping Design

Input: $\mathbf{H}_u[k]$, $\forall u, k$.

1: Initialization: $\mathcal{U} = \{1, \cdots, U\}$, $\mathcal{A} = \{1, \cdots, N_t\}$, $\mathcal{A}_u = \emptyset$, $\forall u$;

2: $\tilde{\mathbf{H}}_u = \left[\mathbf{H}_u^T[1], \mathbf{H}_u^T[2], \cdots, \mathbf{H}_u^T[K]\right]^T$;

3: **while** $|\mathcal{A}|_c > 0$ **do**

4: $\quad \{u^{\mathrm{opt}}, n^{\mathrm{opt}}\} = \arg \max_{u \in \mathcal{U}, n \in \mathcal{A}} \left\|\tilde{\mathbf{H}}_u^{(n)}\right\|_2$;

5: $\quad \mathcal{A}_{u^{\mathrm{opt}}} = \mathcal{A}_{u^{\mathrm{opt}}} \cup \{n^{\mathrm{opt}}\}$;

6: $\quad \mathcal{A} = \mathrm{setdiff}\left(\mathcal{A}, \{n^{\mathrm{opt}}\}\right)$

7: $\quad$ **if** $|\mathcal{A}_u|_c = N_t/U$, **then**

8: $\quad\quad \mathcal{U} = \mathrm{setdiff}\left(\mathcal{U}, \{u^{\mathrm{opt}}\}\right)$;

9: $\quad$ **end if**

10: **end while**

Output: Antenna grouping sets $\mathcal{A}_u$, $\forall u$.

---

5   Simulation Results

In this section, we will investigate the performance of the proposed scheme by numerical simulation. We introduce two benchmarks: (i) the simultaneous greedy hybrid precoding (S-GHP) scheme in [8], and (ii) the design of digital part in [9]. We set $K = 64$ and $D = 16$. For the THz channel model, the number of clusters is assumed to be $N_c = 8$, and each cluster has $N_p = 10$ propagation paths with the angle spreads 7.5°. The azimuth/elevation AoAs and AoDs follow the uniform distribution within $[-\pi/2, \pi/2)$, and each delay-offset is uniformly distributed within $[0, DT_s)$. The "sinc" function is adopted as the pulse shaping filter function $p(\cdot)$. We consider quadrature phase shift keying (QPSK) modulation when conducting BER simulation. The SNR of the system is defined as $10\log_{10}(P/\sigma^2)$ [dB]. The numbers of antennas, RFCs (data streams), and users are provided below each figure.

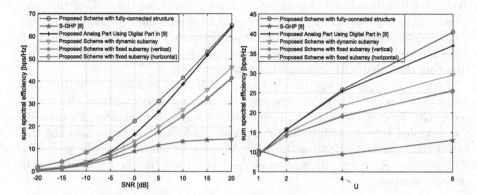

Fig. 3. Sum spectral efficiency achieved by different schemes in an 8-user MIMO system, where $N_t = 16 \times 16$, $N_r = 2 \times 2$, $M_t = 8$, $M_r = N_s = 1$.

Fig. 4. Sum spectral efficiency achieved by different schemes, where $N_t = 16 \times 16$, $N_r = 1$, $M_r = N_s = 1$, $M_t = UN_s$, SNR $= 15$ dB.

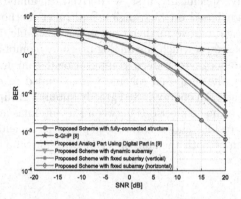

Fig. 5. BER performance achieved by different schemes in a 4-user MIMO system, where $N_t = 16 \times 16$, $N_r = 2 \times 2$, $M_t = 8$, $M_r = N_s = 2$.

Figure 3 illustrates the SSE of proposed schemes against different SNRs. It can be observed that the proposed scheme with fully-connected structure provides a upper-bound for all other schemes, as it requires much more hardware complexity. Also we observe that the proposed scheme and the proposed analog part using digital part in [9] have the same SSE performance in the high SNR. This is because when σ^2 is closed to 0, the proposed digital scheme is equivalent to the digital scheme in [9]. Besides, the proposed scheme with dynamic partially-connected structure outperforms S-GHP scheme [8], the proposed analog part using digital part in [9], and the proposed schemes with different fixed subarray types (vertical and horizontal, cf. [11, Fig. 3]), which indicates that the proposed antenna grouping design improves the precoding performance with dynamic partially-connected structure. Figure 4 illustrates the SSE of the proposed scheme against the number of users. As the number of users increases, the proposed schemes achieve the better performance, and increasing number of users is also better for the proposed scheme with dynamic partially-connected structure than that with different fixed subarray types.

Figure 5 investigates the bit error rate (BER) performance achieved by different schemes. Similarly, We observe that the proposed scheme with fully-connected structure provides a upper-bound for all other schemes. Meanwhile, the proposed scheme with dynamic partially-connected structure also has the better BER performance than the other schemes, benefiting from the proposed HBF scheme which directly minimizes the SMSE between the transmitted and received symbols.

6   Conclusions

This paper proposed an efficient HBF design for multi-user multi-stream communications with THz massive MIMO. By minimizing the SMSE between the transmitted and received symbols, we proposed to design the digital and analog precoding separately. Specifically, first, we derived the analytic solution for digital precoding design based on Lagrangian multiplier method. Then, with the designed digital precoding, we further proposed a tractable criterion for analog precoding design, based on which the analog precoder/combiner are drawn from the pre-defined codebooks to reduce computational complexity and feedback overhead. Moreover, the proposed scheme was extended to dynamic partially-connected architecture. An energy-based greedy antenna grouping algorithm was proposed to optimize the connections between the antennas and radio frequency chains. Simulation results showed that the proposed scheme outperforms its counterparts in term of both the sum spectral efficiency and bit error rate.

References

1. Sarieddeen, H., Alouini, M.S., Al-Naffouri, T.Y.: An overview of signal processing techniques for terahertz communications. Proc. IEEE **109**(10), 1628–1665 (2021)
2. Wan, Z., Gao, Z., Gao, F., Di Renzo, M., Alouini, M.S.: Terahertz massive MIMO with holographic reconfigurable intelligent surfaces. IEEE Trans. Commun. **69**(7), 4732–4750 (2021)
3. Heath, R.W., Gonzalez-Prelcic, N., Rangan, S., Roh, W., Sayeed, A.M.: An overview of signal processing techniques for millimeter wave MIMO systems. IEEE J. Sel. Top. Sig. Process. **10**(3), 436–453 (2016)
4. El Ayach, O., Rajagopal, S., Abu-Surra, S., Pi, Z., Heath, R.W.: Spatially sparse precoding in millimeter wave MIMO systems. IEEE Trans. Wireless Commun. **13**(3), 1499–1513 (2014)
5. Zhang, H., Zhang, H., Dong, J., Leung, V.C., et al.: Energy efficient user clustering and hybrid precoding for terahertz MIMO-NOMA systems. In: ICC 2020–2020 IEEE International Conference on Communications (ICC), pp. 1–5. IEEE (2020)
6. Yuan, H., Yang, N., Yang, K., Han, C., An, J.: Hybrid beamforming for tera-hertz multi-carrier systems over frequency selective fading. IEEE Trans. Commun. **68**(10), 6186–6199 (2020)
7. Yan, L., Han, C., Yuan, J.: A dynamic array-of-subarrays architecture and hybrid precoding algorithms for terahertz wireless communications. IEEE J. Sel. Areas Commun. **38**(9), 2041–2056 (2020)
8. Rodriguez-Fernández, J., Gonzálcz-Prelcic, N.: Low-complexity multiuser hybrid precoding and combining for frequency selective millimeter wave systems. In: 2018 IEEE 19th International Workshop on Signal Processing Advances in Wireless Communications (SPAWC), pp. 1–5. IEEE (2018)
9. Mao, J., Gao, Z., Wu, Y., Alouini, M.S.: Over-sampling codebook-based hybrid minimum sum-mean-square-error precoding for millimeter-wave 3D-MIMO. IEEE Wireless Commun. Lett. **7**(6), 938–941 (2018)
10. Zhang, X.D.: Matrix Analysis and Applications. Cambridge University Press, Cambridge (2017)
11. Sun, Y., et al.: Principal component analysis-based broadband hybrid precoding for millimeter-wave massive MIMO systems. IEEE Trans. Wirel. Commun. **19**(10), 6331–6346 (2020)

Photovoltaic Devices Design Based on Simultaneous Visible-Light Information and Power Transfer Circuits

Jiawei Zhu, Lisu Yu$^{(\boxtimes)}$ (iD), Yong Xia$^{(\boxtimes)}$, Xingjian Wang, Zhenghai Wang, Zhixu Wu, and Yuhao Wang

School of Information Engineering, Nanchang University, Nanchang 330031, China
{lisuyu,xiayong}@ncu.edu.cn

Abstract. In the Internet of Things (IoT) applications based on visible light communication (VLC) systems, such as outdoor intelligent transportation and indoor intelligent home, a large amount of light energy is scattered. Therefore, this paper studies a visible light receiving circuit based on VLC, which is used to collect energy and receive data at the same time to solve such problems, which is called the simultaneous visible-light information and power transfer (SVIPT) circuit. At present, most of the circuits with similar functions to SVIPT are based on two branches, where they are using capacitors to filter direct current (DC) in the data reception branch and inductors to block alternating current (AC) signals at the energy collection end, but these circuits are inefficient and have significant drawbacks that cannot be truly used in practical applications. The SVIPT circuits proposed in this paper discard the previous concept and we have analyzed the main functions of the two branches specifically. Finally, the SVIPT circuit architecture that can be used in the actual scene is designed, and some simulations are carried out to prove its feasibility.

Keywords: Photovoltaic devices · simultaneous visible-light information and power transfer (SVIPT) · energy harvesting · visible light communication (VLC) · receiving circuit

1 Introduction

Today, the Internet of Things (IoT) is becoming more and more common in our daily lives. Home appliances, furniture, wearables and outdoor intelligent transportation are seamlessly connected to the Internet to exchange information for proper operation, with the ultimate goal of improving our lives by monitoring and controlling the environment around us [1]. The deployment speed of IoT products is very fast, increasing from 9 billion in 2013 to more than 20 billion in 2022, and will continue to increase with the huge market demand. This growth will bring more than 100 billion dollars of opportunities to the healthcare, intelligent home, intelligent transportation, public utilities and consumer electronics markets. To enable true thing-to-thing information transfer, IoT

J. Zhao (Ed.): WiSATS 2023, LNICST 509, pp. 74–84, 2023.
https://doi.org/10.1007/978-3-031-34851-8_6

devices must have a wireless means of communication, as unconstrained devices can be easily integrated into everyday objects, especially if they can be placed in areas that are inaccessible to people. In addition, IoT devices should be able to harvest energy from their environment to avoid frequent manual charging or regular battery replacement [2], and most of all to save available resources and maximize the energy use of available resources [3].

Visible light communication (VLC) [4] technology is developing rapidly in the world today to generate the Internet of Lights (IoL) scenario, so this technology generally transmits information by switching frequencies that cannot be detected by human eyes, and will not interfere with the normal operation of other equipment [5]. If VLC is used for information exchange between things, it is possible to use light for both data transmission and lighting [6]. The most important thing is that this kind of IoT communication can complete information transmission at some low transmission rates [7]. The general VLC system is not only vulnerable to the impact of the external environment light, but most of the light emitted by the system will be scattered, resulting in a waste of resources. IoT devices equipped with photovoltaic-type devices [8] can not only collect light energy from LED lights and the external environment, but also receive optically encoded information, and the external ambient light has less influence on the signal reception of photovoltaic devices [9]. In VLC based on photovoltaic devices, energy collection and data reception are carried out simultaneously. At the same time, for intelligent transportation systems similar to VLC, when outdoor sunlight and LED signal light sources overlap, the response rate of photovoltaic devices remains good [10]. Under the same outdoor environmental conditions, the bit error rate of photovoltaic devices is lower than that of photodiodes (PIN) and avalanche diodes (APD) detectors, and when conducting VLC outdoors, photovoltaic devices will generate more electrical energy for storage or power supply to subsequent circuits.

At present, the dual receiving circuits of photovoltaic devices based on VLC are mostly based on two model branches, one for data reception and the other for energy collection [11]. Capacitors are used in the data reception branch to block direct current (DC), and choke inductors are used in the energy harvesting branch to filter out useful signals and let DC signals pass through. However, a disadvantage of this method is that it requires a very large choke inductor and a relatively large space footprint. The resistance is used to simulate the energy collection load. Although the resistance provides a good first-order load approximation for energy collection, it cannot capture high-order effects, and the resistance cannot collect energy. The most important thing is that the voltage at both ends of the photovoltaic devices is very unstable, and it is easy to be affected by light, which will have a certain impact on the subsequent energy storage. This model branch has obvious disadvantages and cannot be used directly in VLC. To further solve the existing defects, this paper relates to a kind of circuit of simultaneous visible-light information and power transfer (SVIPT) based on energy collection and data reception of photovoltaic devices [12], and it is mainly used to save resources by collecting the remaining light energy when the VLC is carried out and absorbing the external ambient light when the VLC is not carried out [13]. The main advantage of the designed circuit is the materialization of the two branches. In the energy collection branch, a boost circuit is used to stabilize the voltage rise at both ends of the photovoltaic devices at a certain value, and then it is transported to the supercapacitor for energy storage and power supply to the amplifier in signal transmission. In the data receiving branch, a current sensing resistor is used to sense the useful signal and transport the subsequent processing circuit, which systematically solves the practicability of the energy collection and data receiving circuit based on VLC.

2 Principle of Photovoltaic Devices Model

Compared with PIN tubes and APD tubes, photovoltaic devices are increasingly used in VLC systems, which do not require external bias and rely on their built-in electric field for signal transmission, and generate excess power while doing so. Even though the large capacitance of the photovoltaic devices will directly lead to the response speed of the device itself, the large receiving area of the photovoltaic devices makes it have a stronger light capture capability. In addition, the main thing is that IoT based on VLC does not need a high-speed transmission rate like intelligent homes and general photovoltaic devices can meet its communication needs.

2.1 Photovoltaic Devices Model for Energy Harvesting

Most of the commercially available photovoltaic devices are PN junction structures, so when the photovoltaic devices are used as an energy harvesting device its equivalent circuit is shown in Fig. 1, with R_L denoting the load. The DC model of photovoltaic devices can be seen as consisting of a constant current source, a diode, a compound resistor and a series resistor. According to the equivalent model, the relationship between the output current and voltage of the photovoltaic devices can be derived as [14]:

$$I_{pv} = I_{ph} - I_d - \frac{V_{pv} + I_{pv}R_s}{R_{sh}} \qquad (1)$$

where I_{pv} and V_{pv} are the output current and output voltage of the photovoltaic devices, I_{ph} is the constant current source current, R_s is the series resistor, and R_{sh} is the compound resistor. I_d is the diode forward current, the value of which can be calculated by the following equation:

$$I_d = I_0 exp[\frac{q(V_{pv} + I_{pv}R_s)}{NAkT} - 1] \qquad (2)$$

where I_0 denotes the reverse saturation current of the diode, q is the charge of an electron, N is the number of photovoltaic devices in series, A is the diode ideal factor, k is the Boltzmann constant, and T is the Kelvin temperature.

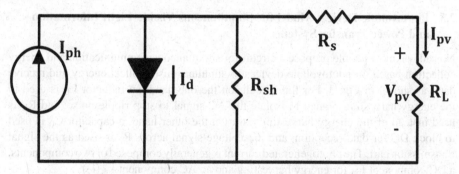

Fig. 1. Photovoltaic devices model for energy harvesting.

2.2 Photovoltaic Devices Model for Communication Systems

When photovoltaic devices are used for information transmission, their alternating current (AC) equivalent model is shown in Fig. 2. For photovoltaic devices, large internal capacitance cannot be ignored, so a capacitor C_S and a parallel resistance R_{sh} are used to equivalent the internal capacitance effect of photovoltaic devices. A small signal equivalent resistance r is used to replace the diode, and a series inductor L is added to simulate the inductance at the connection of the photovoltaic devices, and capacitor C is used to block the DC signal to let the AC signal with information pass through. From the above description, it is clear that the frequency response of the photovoltaic devices used for communication systems is given by the following equation [15]:

$$\left|\frac{V(\omega)}{I_{ph}(\omega)}\right|^2 = \left|\frac{\frac{R_L}{R_X}}{\frac{1}{r} + j\omega C_S + \frac{1}{R_{sh}} + \frac{1}{R_X}}\right|^2 \tag{3}$$

where ω is the angular frequency, and j is an imaginary number. R_X denotes the total resistance value of R_s, inductor L, capacitor C_0 and load R_L, whose expression is:

$$R_X = R_s + j\omega L + \frac{1}{j\omega C_0} + R_L \tag{4}$$

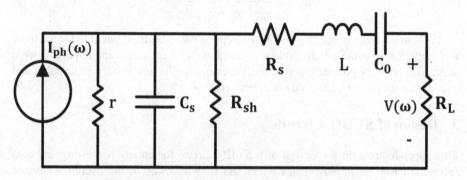

Fig. 2. Photovoltaic devices model for communication.

2.3 Photovoltaic Devices Model for Simultaneous Visible-Light Information and Power Transfer Systems

Nowadays, most people propose a circuit for simultaneous communication and energy collection based on photovoltaic devices to simultaneously collect energy and receive data, as shown in Fig. 3. For this circuit, on the one hand, an inductor L_0 is used in the energy harvesting branch to isolate the AC signal to stop ripple noise, and R_L is used instead of the energy harvesting part. On the other hand, a capacitor C_0 is used to block DC for data reception, and the voltage signal across R_c is used as the signal transmission part. The photogenerated current is generally composed of two components, a DC component I_{ph} for energy harvesting and an AC component $I_{ph}(\omega)$.

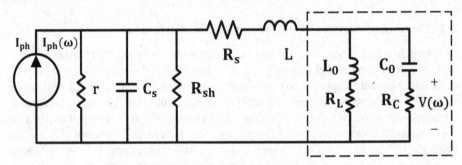

Fig. 3. Photovoltaic devices model for SVIPT circuits.

for signal transmission action. The frequency response of its entire structure can be calculated by the following equation [16]:

$$\left|\frac{V(\omega)}{I_{ph}(\omega)}\right|^2 = \left|\frac{\frac{R_{LC}}{R_s+j\omega L+R_{LC}} * \frac{R_C}{1/j\omega C_0+R_C}}{\frac{1}{r} + \frac{1}{1/j\omega C_s} + \frac{1}{R_{sh}} + \frac{1}{R_s+j\omega L+R_{LC}}}\right|^2 \tag{5}$$

R_{LC} represents the sum of the parallel network resistances of the two branches for energy collection and data reception, which is expressed as:

$$R_{LC} = \frac{1}{\frac{1}{j\omega L_0+R_L} + \frac{1}{1/j\omega C_0+R_C}} \tag{6}$$

Although energy collection and data reception can be carried out at the same time, this method is extremely vulnerable to external noise interference and requires a large space. The most important thing is that the energy collection voltage is unstable and energy storage cannot be carried out effectively.

3 Design of SVIPT Circuits

This paper focuses on the design of a SVIPT circuit for energy harvesting and data reception based on photovoltaic devices. As shown in Fig. 4, the overall schematic diagram of this circuit structure is placed on the whole visible light system. On the one hand, at the transmitter side, the encoded signal is superimposed with the LED drive signal to control the bright and dark changes of the LED, which does not affect the lighting because the signal transmission rate is so fast that the human eye cannot discern the changes in the brightness of the LED. On the other hand, at the receiving end, the photovoltaic devices receive the signal from the LED and the external ambient light, and the photocurrent generated is partly converted into the voltage at both ends by the current sensing resistor, and partly stored in the supercapacitor through the boost circuit for subsequent power supply to the receiving chip.

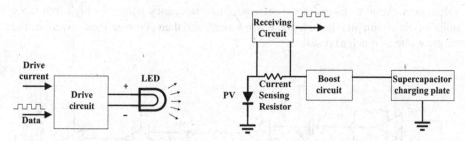

Fig. 4. Diagram of the entire VLC structure using the SVIPT circuit.

This circuit mainly consists of modules such as photovoltaic type devices, a current sensing resistor, boost circuits, a supercapacitor charging board, instrument amplifier circuits, bandpass filter circuits, comparison circuits and reference level circuits [17], etc. And the specific circuit is shown in Fig. 5. The current sensing resistor is generally very small, about a few ohms, and its main role is to convert the current signal into a voltage signal across the current sense resistor and then transmitted it to the instrument amplifier circuit. The instrument amplifier circuit is mainly used to convert the voltage signals at both ends of the current induction resistance into unidirectional signals and amplify them in a certain proportion, and the amplification factor is given by the following equation:

$$G = 5 + 5\frac{R5}{R4} \tag{7}$$

The instrument amplifier chip used in this circuit is the INA322 from Texas Instruments, which is suitable for this circuit due to its low power consumption and low price. After the instrument amplifier circuit, the signal is then transmitted to a band-pass filter and compared with the reference circuit to restore the originally transmitted signal, and the main function of the band-pass filter is to filter out the very low frequencies in the signal and the high-frequency noise generated by the external environment and the circuit, retaining only the useful signal. The bandwidth of the bandpass oscilloscope of this circuit is shown in Fig. 6. Respectively, the amplifier chips used in the bandpass filter circuit and the comparison circuit are OPA2340 and TLV7011.

Compared with other energy collection and data-receiving model circuits, this circuit does not use a choke inductor to filter out useful signals on the energy collection branch, nor does it use resistance to simulate the energy collection load. Instead, it uses a low-power boost chip to raise the voltage of the photovoltaic device to a certain value, i.e

3.3 V, so that the voltage can be stabilized before charging the subsequent supercapacitor charging plate. By controlling the resistance values of R2 and R3, the voltage value after boosting can be changed, and the numbers of all chips in this circuit and their performance parameters are shown in Table 1. The charging and discharging circuit of the supercapacitor is simpler than that of the battery, and the supercapacitor is small in size, saving space. What's more, the subsequent supercapacitor can also provide energy for those operational amplifier chips. On the data-receiving branch, instead of blocking the DC signal with a capacitor, the current sensing resistor senses the current change and converts it into the voltage signal at both ends, which is then amplified and filtered by the subsequent circuit to filter out the extremely low-frequency noise, the high-frequency noise of the circuit and the external environment, and then compare them to reduce the bit error rate as much as possible.

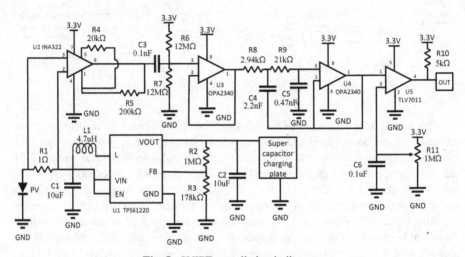

Fig. 5. SVIPT overall circuit diagram.

Table 1. Performance parameters of the chip used.

Chip Number	Chip Name	Supply Voltage	Conversion Efficiency	Voltage Noise (1 kHz)	Quiescent Current
U1	TPS61220		Up to 95%		5.5 uA
U2	INA322	3.3 V		100 nV $\sqrt{Hz}$	40 uA
U3 and U4	OPA2340	3.3 V		25 nV $\sqrt{Hz}$	750 uA
U5	TLV7011	3.3 V		75 nV $\sqrt{Hz}$	5 uA

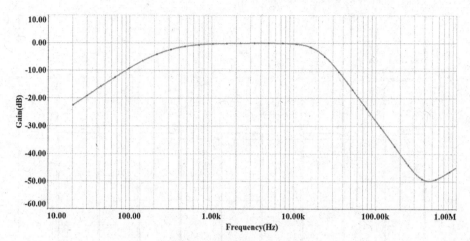

Fig. 6. Bandwidth of this circuit.

4 Results and Discussions

General silicon solar cells have high photoelectric conversion efficiency. When silicon photovoltaic devices are used as visible light detectors in SVIPT circuits, the voltages at both ends of the detectors can be effectively boosted and transmitted encoded digital signals. For example, when transmitting a 1 kHz square wave signal [18], the signal output image is shown in Fig. 7. As can be seen, at the signal output, the 1 kHz square wave signal is converted into a voltage signal after passing through the current sensing resistor and passed to the subsequent circuit for further processing. Although the signal after the bandpass filter is slightly miscoded and distorted, the transmitted square wave signal can be output more completely after adjusting the resistance value of the sliding resistor of the reference level circuit. For the energy harvesting module, adjust the resistance value of R2 and R3 so that the final voltage reaches about 3.3 V, as shown in Fig. 8. Although the output voltage will have some ripple noise, it is within a certain controllable range and will not affect the supercapacitor for energy storage.

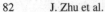

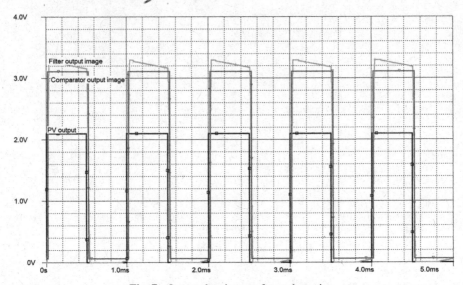

Fig. 7. Output data images for each section.

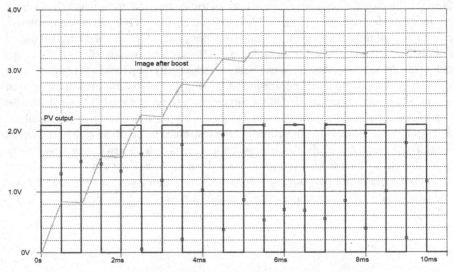

Fig. 8. Boost branch simulation results.

5   Conclusion

To save available resources, we have designed a SVIPT circuit in a VLC system based on photovoltaic devices. In this circuit, for the data transmission branch, we discarded the conventional concept of using a capacitor to filter out the direct flow AC and instead used a current sensing resistor to convert the current signal with information into a voltage signal before transporting it to the back circuit. For the energy harvesting branch, a low-power booster chip is used to boost the photovoltaic device to a certain voltage before powering the supercapacitor. There is a small amount of ripple noise, but it is within the acceptable range. We have simulated this circuit to verify its feasibility, and the circuit takes up little space and can be easily integrated into small VLC systems indoors and outdoors. This circuit can largely reduce the frequency of battery replacement and further reduce the occurrence of emergencies when performing some high-risk work such as underwater communication and inaccessible areas for human beings, so this circuit is of high practical value for VLC in future IoL scenarios.

References

1. Li, J., Liu, A., Shen, G., Li, L., et al.: Retro-VLC: enabling battery-free duplex visible light communication for mobile and IoT applications. In: Proceedings of the 16th International Workshop on Mobile Computing Systems and Applications, pp. 21–26, Santa Fe New Mexico, USA. IEEE (2015)
2. S. Ramos, I., Demirkol, J., Paradells, D., Vössing, K. M., et al.: Towards energy-autonomous wake-up receiver using visible light communication. In: 13th IEEE Annual Consumer Communications & Networking Conference CCNC, Las Vegas - United States, pp. 544–549. IEEE (2016)
3. Sarker, M.R., Saad, M.H.M., Olazagoitia, J.L., Vinolas, J.: Review of power converter impact of electromagnetic energy harvesting circuits and devices for autonomous sensor applications. Electronics **10**(9), 1108 (2021)
4. Yu, L., Liu, Z., Wen, M., et al.: Sparse code multiple access for 6G wireless communication networks: recent advances and future directions. IEEE Commun. Stand. Mag. **5**(2), 92–99 (2021)
5. Zhan, S., Yu, L., Wang, Z., et al.: Cell traffic prediction based on convolutional neural network for software-defined ultra-dense visible light communication networks. Secur. Commun. Networks (2021)
6. Chen, X., Min, C., Guo, J.: Visible light communication system using silicon photocell for energy gathering and data receiving. Int. J. Opt. (2017)
7. Malik, B., Zhang, X.: Solar panel receiver system implementation for visible light communication. In: 2015 IEEE International Conference on Electronics, Circuits, and Systems ICECS, Cairo, Egypt, pp. 502–503. IEEE (2015)
8. Lee, S.H.: A passive transponder for visible light identification using a solar cell. IEEE Sens. J. **15**(10), 5398–5403 (2015)
9. Pradana, A., Ahmadi, N., Adionos, T.: Design and implementation of visible light communication system using pulse width modulation. In: 2015 International Conference on Electrical Engineering and Informatics ICEEI, Denpasar, Indonesia, pp. 25–30. IEEE (2015)
10. Hande, A., Polk, T., Walker, W., Bhatia, D.: Indoor solar energy harvesting for sensor network router nodes. Microprocess. Microsyst. **31**(6), 420–432 (2007)
11. Shin, W.H., Yang, S.H., Kwon, D.H., et al.: Self-reverse-biased solar panel optical receiver for simultaneous visible light communication and energy harvesting. Opt. Express **24**(22), A1300–A1305 (2016)
12. Varshney, A., Soleiman, A., Mottola, L., Voigt, T.: Battery-free visible light sensing. In: Proceedings of the 4th ACM Workshop on Visible Light Communication Systems, UT, USA, pp. 3–8. ACM (2017)

13. Tavakkolnia, I., Jagadamma, L.K., Bian, R., et al.: Organic photovoltaics for simultaneous energy harvesting and high-speed MIMO optical wireless communications. Light: Sci. Appl. **10**(1), 1–11 (2021)
14. Zhao, W., Kamezaki, M., Yamaguchi, K., Konno, M., et al.: An experimental analysis of pipe inspection using solar panel receiver for visible light communication and energy harvesting. In: 2020 IEEE/ASME International Conference on Advanced Intelligent Mechatronics AIM, Boston, USA, pp. 1848–1853. IEEE (2020)
15. Mitra, A., Srivastava, A., Bohara, V.A., Solanki, D.: Experimental validation of optical wireless receiver using solar panel with bandwidth enhancement circuit. In: IEEE 95th Vehicular Technology Conference VTC2022-Spring, USA, pp. 1–6. IEEE (2022)
16. Wang, Z., Tsonev, D., Videv, S., et al.: On the design of a solar-panel receiver for optical wireless communications with simultaneous energy harvesting. IEEE J. Sel. Areas Commun. **33**(8), 1612–1623 (2015)
17. Gupta, A., Singh, V., Gautam, M., Dixit, A.: Design and Implementation for a Duplex Visible Light Communication Link. In: 14th International Conference on Communication Systems & NETworkS COMSNETS, pp. 190–193. IEEE (2022)
18. Xu, X., Shen, Y., Yang, J., Xu, C., et al.: Passive VLC: enabling practical visible light backscatter communication for battery-free IoT applications. In: Proceedings of the 23rd Annual International Conference on Mobile Computing and Networking, pp. 180–192. Snowbird, UT, USA (2017)

Marketing in Wireless Communication: A Systematic Review

Angelie Natalia Sanjaya[1] , Agung Purnomo[1] , Yogi Tri Prasetyo[2](✉) ,
Cuk Tho[1] , Fairuz Iqbal Maulana[1] , and Satria Fadil Persada[1]

[1] Bina Nusantara University, Jakarta 11480, Indonesia
[2] Mapua University, 1002 Manila, Philippines
ytprasetyo@mapua.edu.ph

Abstract. Wireless communication is becoming a trend in today's environment because it facilitates access to a wider range than non-wireless communication. In entrepreneurship, the product marketing process will greatly benefit if it is carried out with the right STP strategy. In addition to creating efficiencies in marketing mix activities, it also expands the reach of consumers and becomes more sophisticated. With this research study, we review the literature and relevant research data on marketing in wireless communication. In particular, we report a systematic literature review applying the PRISMA guidelines. There were 21 relevant articles on wireless communications and marketing published based on a systematic search of the Scopus database. The results show that publications on marketing in wireless communication have not been widely analyzed with various levels, quantitative, industries, and perspectives. The top research country was the United States and the most widely used stratified analysis was the network level. Industry analysis contains mostly information technology topics using a positioning and process perspective. Further research is possible, such as research into marketing in wireless communications using team levels with energy or food industry topics and a marketing element perspective, targeting, price, and place.

Keywords: Entrepreneurship · Marketing · Marketing Mix · Systematic Literature Review · Wireless Communication

1 Introduction

Wireless communication has progressed and increased the number of people using mobile devices [1]. Each service provides added value to customers, which makes the service easier to use [2]. Equipped with internet services, wireless communication provides an unprecedented level of convenience for customers [3]. One example proposes a new transaction scheme to significantly improve customer security [4]. Communication in entrepreneurship will continue to develop [5] representing the growing human responsibility for business and marketing [6]. This is very useful, especially in terms of marketing, because the benefits perceived by customers greatly affect attitudes toward

© ICST Institute for Computer Sciences, Social Informatics and Telecommunications Engineering 2023
Published by Springer Nature Switzerland AG 2023. All Rights Reserved
J. Zhao (Ed.): WiSATS 2023, LNICST 509, pp. 85–93, 2023.
https://doi.org/10.1007/978-3-031-34851-8_7

product marketing [7]. Wireless communication can access a wider range so that marketing strategies can also be significantly improved. Of all the studies, there has been no research that studies marketing in wireless communication using a Systematic Literature Review approach.

A systematic Literature Review (SLR) is a research method that identifies and synthesizes a subject area or topic by collecting relevant data [8]. This study uses qualitative data collection methods from previous studies from Scopus sources as a reference for observations [9]. The protocol used along with descriptions and notes of the steps for taking documents, documents excluded or included, and stages of analysis are also attached [10]. The question posed in this research study is, what is the state of the existing literature and research on marketing in wireless communications? From a systematic literature review point of view, this study aims to transparently review literature and research on marketing in wireless communications.

2   Methods

In this study, the Preferred Reporting Items for Systematic Review and Meta-Analyses (PRISMA) guidelines were used and carried out in a systematic literature review. A large literature database was subjected to a literature search for complete information. We have linked keywords related to wireless communication and marketing to find and link to relevant articles in the global Scopus database. The Scopus database was used as the main source of information by scientists, as it was considered an authoritative source of scientific research. This study uses the keywords "wireless communication" and "marketing" in the title, abstract, and author keywords to retrieve relevant data from the Scopus database, as shown in Fig. 1. Data mining was limited to annual data as it collects one year of published data. The search query options used in data mining were (TITLE-ABS-KEY ("wireless communication") AND TITLE-ABS-KEY (marketing)) AND (LIMIT-TO (SUBJAREA, "BUSI")) AND (LIMIT-TO (SRCTYPE, "j")) as of October 2022. We discovered 21 articles in this stage.

This SLR uses analysis of quantitative, industry, multilevel, and perspective. The quantitative analysis consists of annual publications and geographical contexts [5, 6, 9]. The multilevel analysis includes levels of individual, team, company, network, and institutional. The industry analysis includes information technology, services, manufacturing, energy, and food [8]. The perspective analysis includes segmenting, targeting, positioning, and marketing mix 7P's [11].

3   Results and Discussion

In this study of marketing in wireless communication, the current status of the literature and previous research has been described based on analysis of quantitative, industry, multilevel, and perspective.

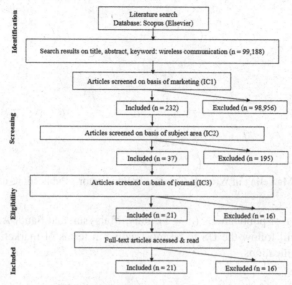

Fig. 1. PRISMA Protocols.

3.1 Publications of the Year

Figure 2 presents the 21 documents that have been published each year. Scopus database records show publications started in 1991 with one publication. However, in 1992 and 1993, no publication was recorded. In 1994 there was one publication and between 1995 and 1999 there was no publication. Then, in 2000 there was one publication but in 2001 and 2022 there were no more publications. There were publications in 2003 but no publications from 2004 until 2006. Then, there were publications in 2007 with two publications, decreased by one publication in the following year 2009. The publication with an increasing growth rate and the peak of publication annuals was in 2010. However, 2011 came down with one publication. Up slightly with two publications in 2012. From 2013 to 2015 stagnant with one publication per year. There were no publications recorded in the period 2016 to 2019. Then, there has been a resurgence of one publication every year in 2020 and 2021.

Based on these data, it can be seen that the number of publications related to marketing in wireless communication has an unstable, increasing, and decreasing growth. Marketing in wireless communication has become a trend because it offers effective solutions to communicate marketing activities, especially in the business world, so that it can reach a wider range of consumers and become easier to access [12].

3.2 Geographical Contexts

15 countries have studied marketing in wireless communications (see Fig. 3). The United States was the top research country for marketing publications in wireless communications (n = 12). Then followed by Italy (n = 3), Malaysia (n = 3), and Saudi Arabia (n = 2). Canada, China, Hong Kong, Jordan, Singapore, Taiwan, United Kingdom have

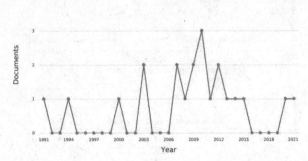

Fig. 2. The Marketing in Wireless Communication Sector's Publications of The Year.

the same number of publications (n = 1). Italy, Malaysia, and Saudi Arabia were the countries that will follow the US to be most active in terms of marketing research in wireless communications.

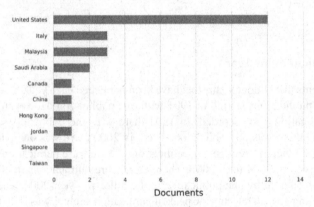

Fig. 3. Region Number of Annual Publication of Marketing in Wireless Communication

Publications on marketing in wireless communication have been researched by various countries and are not dominated by certain countries.

3.3 Multilevel and Industry Analysis

Research on marketing in wireless communication can be analyzed using multilevel and industry analysis as shown in Table 1. There were five levels of multilevel analysis and five types of industry which were the main emphasis of the studies examined [8]. Most of the publications included in this study examine wireless communication in the context of marketing by taking a network-level analysis, totaling eight articles. Four publications concentrate on the individual analysis level, two concentrates on the team level, four on the firm level, and three on the institutional level.

In the first individual-level analysis, the author discusses the email system which was considered to be the world's premier online service [2]. The second and third authors discuss marketing electronic media becoming more accessible and moving towards wider adoption [12] and want to drive more sales with new marketing strategies such as turning trucks into "mobile billboards" [13]. The fourth author examines imaginative companies designed to deliver targets quickly and at a low cost [14].

Two publications used team-level multilevel analysis. These articles examine the interaction of voice and SMS services provided by wireless carriers [15] which Network Management will take over in the next few years [16].

The next four articles were analyzed using the multilevel firm level. The first article explores the needs of m-commerce customers for direct marketing in the mobile environment [17]. The next article discusses increasing value-added services such as mobile broadband internet services, video streaming, etc. for postpaid subscribers [18]. The next article examines that the innovation process in this global industry is "not globalized" as a whole [19], so companies can imagine to see various possibilities and create competitive advantages [20].

Table 1. Multilevel Analysis and Industry Analysis of Marketing in Wireless Communication.

Analysis of Industry & Multilevel	Individual	Team	Firm	Network	Institutional
Information Technology	[2]	[15, 16]	[17]	[1, 3, 7, 21]	[22]
Services	[12, 13]		[18]		[4]
Manufacturing	[14]			[23–26]	
Energy			[19, 20]		
Food					[27]

Then, there were eight publications on wireless communications that analyze marketing at the network level. The first article identifies stakeholder perceptions and behaviors that can influence the success of commercialization [21]. The next article examines the effect of convenience on shopping intentions through mobile communication devices [3], then continues with an investigation of consumer factors when adopting m-commerce [1]. The next article suggests that perceived usefulness, consumer innovation, and personal attachment affect mobile marketing [7]. Then several articles predict the determinants that influence consumer expectations and intentions for marketing [23] and mobile commerce [24], examine the factors that affect consumer acceptance of mobile marketing in two global markets [25], using the Unified Theory of Acceptance Model and Use of Technology 2 (UTAUT2) [26].

There were three publications in this study taking institutional-level analysis. These articles propose a blind equalization algorithm to classify data by unsupervised learning [22], a Secure M-Commerce System (SMCS) scheme to improve the security of online shopping with credit card transactions [4], as well as the development of a decision-making model for distribution strategy [27].

Research on marketing in wireless communication can be analyzed using an industrial approach [8]. There were nine publications in the information technology industry. The service industry has been studied through four documents. Also, there were five studies reviewing the manufacturing industry. The energy industry can be identified from two publications. Then, there was one publication reviewing the food industry.

There were several research gaps in marketing studies in wireless communications. First, service industry research has not been linked to team and network analysis. Second, the manufacturing industry has also not been linked to team, firm, and institutional analysis. Third, research in the energy industry has only recently been linked to firm analysis, while individual, team, network, and institutional analyzes have not been linked. Not much different from the food industry which was still new in terms of institutional analysis. The least researched levels of multilevel analysis for marketing in wireless communications are the team levels. The least studied industries for marketing in wireless communications were energy and food.

3.4 Perspective Analysis

In addition to analysis using multilevel and industry analysis, research on wireless communication can also be analyzed from a marketing perspective as shown in table 2. There were two factors from a marketing perspective, STP and Marketing Mix 7P which will be the main emphasis of the study being researched. The STP perspective describes the customer identification process to optimize its product value offering. Meanwhile, the Marketing Mix 7P's perspective can be considered as a process of designing, communicating, and delivering customer value with different tactical attributes [11].

Publications related to this research on STP perspective, mostly examine wireless communication in the context of marketing by taking positioning perspective analysis in the marketing process. Seven publications concentrate on the perspective of segmentation analysis. These articles investigate consumer behavior towards the adoption of m-commerce products [1], mobile commerce products [24], marketing of mobile in global markets [25], people's behavioral intentions as m-TV users [26], as well as perceptions and behaviors towards the success of advanced technological processes [21]. The next article contains psychographic conditions against physical evidence that considers email as the main online service in today's world [2]. Recent articles suggest that the physical evidence of market demand is shifting so that technical expertise is growing in some geographic areas [19].

Then five publications concentrate on the perspective of targeting analysis. These articles focus on the benefits of products by providing a level of convenience for online shopping via mobile communication devices [3]. The second article measures the usefulness of mobile information/programs for marketing [7]. The third article focuses on direct marketing in the mobile m-commerce environment thus exploring customer needs [17]. The next article suggests a difference so that the company's marketing becomes faster by breaking away from the conventional market and serving a wider reach [14]. The last article focuses on its efforts to improve its presence process and offer value-added services [18].

Next is a discussion from the positioning perspective which has the largest number of studies. These articles describe some of the differences in the product market regarding the relationship between individual-level characteristics, attitudes, and mobile marketing activities [23]. The next article would like to offer a solution for more sales with a "moving billboard" promotion strategy [13] and a one-to-one promotion strategy

Table 2. Perspective Analysis of Marketing in Wireless Communication.

Marketing Mix 7P's	STP Analysis		
	Segmenting	Targeting	Positioning
Product	[1, 24]	[3]	[23]
Price			
Promotion	[25]	[7, 14, 17]	[12, 13]
Place			
People	[26]		
Process	[21]	[18]	[4, 15, 16, 22, 27]
Physical Evidence	[2, 19]		[20]

[12]. Subsequent articles develop network management processes from non-wireless to emerging services [16], develop process blind equalization algorithms [22], improve online shopping security processes with secure m-commerce schemes [4], develop process retrieval models decisions for product distribution strategies [27], as well as developing economies of scale with physical evidence of a single business model as broad as possible [20].

Research on marketing in wireless communication can be analyzed using a marketing mix 7P's approach. There were four publications on the product topic. The promotion topic has been studied through six documents. Also, there was one study reviewing the people topic. The topic of the process can be identified from seven publications. Then, there were three publications reviewing the physical evidence topic.

There were some gaps in wireless communication research using a marketing perspective. The perspective of people has not been associated with the perspective of targeting and positioning. The physical evidence perspective has not been linked to the targeting perspective. The least researched analysis of the STP perspective for marketing in wireless communications was the targeting element. Then, the analysis of the Marketing Mix 7P's perspective that has never been studied was the price and place elements.

4   Conclusions

Marketing and its strategy are important elements in promoting the development of wireless communication. Marketing and dissemination of information about a product's value can be carried out in a wider and smoother market reach using wireless communication. This study focuses on obtaining information that ultimately research findings can be utilized related to marketing in wireless communication by providing some quantitative analysis in the related literature. The quantitative analysis carried out in this study was the annual publication and geographic location. In addition, this study presents the results of multilevel analysis (individuals, teams, companies, networks, and institutions), industry analysis (information technology, services, manufacturing, energy, and food), as well as analysis of marketing perspectives (STP elements and marketing mix). The results of this study indicate that marketing in wireless communications has been studied in various industry fields and perspectives. Annual publications show that research trends in the field have unstable growth. However, in recent years, marketing publications in wireless communication have increased. The United States was the leading research country that has published twelve articles on marketing in wireless communications. The most frequently reviewed multilevel analysis of this topic was the network level with eight articles. In industrial analysis, information technology was a topic of discussion that was often transported. Then, the most widely discussed marketing perspective was in the positioning element of the marketing process.

Further research that has the opportunity to be carried out, especially for marketing research in wireless communication, is to use the team level by connecting the topics of the energy and food industries. Marketing studies in wireless communication with the topic of targeting, price, and place have the opportunity to be studied. The study of digital marketing in wireless communication using the metaverse and web 3.0 is also interesting. This study has limitations in using published data based on the Scopus database. It is hoped that this research can provide avenues for new research from the perspective of partial knowledge and advanced analytics.

Acknowledgment. This research was funded by Mapúa University Directed Research for Innovation and Value Enhancement (DRIVE).

References

1. Chong, A.Y.L., Chan, F.T.S., Ooi, K.B.: Predicting consumer decisions to adopt mobile commerce: cross country empirical examination between China and Malaysia. Decis. Support Syst. **53**, 34–43 (2012). https://doi.org/10.1016/j.dss.2011.12.001
2. Giussani, B.: I want my wireless email! Total Telecom. 13 (2003)
3. Jih, W.J.: Effects of consumer-perceived convenience on shopping intention in mobile commerce: an empirical study. Int. J. E-Business Res. (IJEBR) **3**, 33–48 (2007). https://doi.org/10.4018/jebr.2007100102
4. Leu, F.Y., Huang, Y.L., Wang, S.M.: A Secure M-Commerce System based on credit card transaction. Electron Commer. Res. Appl. **14**, 351–360 (2015). https://doi.org/10.1016/j.elerap.2015.05.001
5. Purnomo, A., Firdaus, M., Sari, Y.K.P., Azzahira, Z.: A Retrospective of the business communication using bibliometric review. In: Proceedings of the International Conference on Industrial Engineering and Operations Management, pp. 729–730 (2021)
6. Purnomo, A., Herman, R.T., Asitah, N.: Green marketing publication: bibliometric perspective mapping. In: Proceedings of the International Conference on Industrial Engineering and Operations Management, pp. 1772–1781 (2021)
7. Rohm, A.J., Gao, T., Sultan, F., Pagani, M.: Brand in the hand: a cross-market investigation of consumer acceptance of mobile marketing. Bus Horiz. **55**, 485–493 (2012). https://doi.org/10.1016/j.bushor.2012.05.004
8. Andreini, D., Bettinelli, C.: Business Model Innovation: From Systematic Literature Review to Future Research Directions. Springer International Publishing, Cham (2017). https://doi.org/10.1007/978-3-319-53351-3

9. Purnomo, A., Asitah, N., Firdausi, N., Putra, S.W., Raya, M.K.F.: A study of digital marketing research using bibliometric analysis. In: Proceedings of 2021 International Conference on Information Management and Technology, ICIMTech 2021, pp. 807–812 (2021). https://doi.org/10.1109/ICIMTECH53080.2021.9535086

10. PRISMA, https://prisma-statement.org/. Accessed 13 Oct 2022

11. Kotler, P., Keller, K.L., Chernev, A.: Marketing management. Pearson Education (2022)

12. Klabjan, D., Pei, J.: In-store one-to-one marketing. J. Retail. Consum. Serv. 18, 64–73 (2011). https://doi.org/10.1016/j.jretconser.2010.09.012

13. Marchetti, M.: Qualcomm's road. Sales and Marketing. Management 152, 90 (2000)

14. Hamel, G., Prahalad, C.K.: Corporate imagination and expeditionary marketing. Harv Bus Rev. 69, 81–92 (1991)

15. Kim, Y., Telang, R., Vogt, W.B., Krishnan, R.: An empirical analysis of mobile voice service and SMS: a structural model. Manage Sci. 56, 234–252 (2010). https://doi.org/10.1287/mnsc.1090.1091

16. Janakiram, V.K., Chandra, R., Kripalani, A.T., Rudrapatna, A.N., Russell, J.E.: Network management needs for the wireless communication environment. J. Netw. Syst. Manage. 2, 7–27 (1994). https://doi.org/10.1007/BF02141602

17. Cudmore, B.A., Patton, J.R.: The intimate marketer: Personalized direct marketing strategies in a wireless environment. J. Int. Comm. 6, 73–96 (2008). https://doi.org/10.1080/15332860802086243

18. Al-Ghamdi, S.M.: Mobily of UAE: Penetrating Saudi Arabia - A global case study. J. Global Business Adv. 3, 295–312 (2010). https://doi.org/10.1504/JGBA.2010.036035

19. Macher, J.T., Mowery, D.C., di Minin, A.: The "non-globalization" of innovation in the semiconductor industry. Calif Manage Rev. 50, 217–242 (2007). https://doi.org/10.2307/41166425

20. Ghemawat, P.: The Forgotten Strategy. Harv Bus Rev. 81, 76–84 (2003)

21. Bunn, M.D., Azmi, F., Puentes, M.: Stakeholder perceptions and implications for technology marketing in multi-sector innovations: The case of intelligent transport systems. Int. J. Technol. Mark. 4, 129–148 (2009). https://doi.org/10.1504/IJTMKT.2009.026866

22. Li, Y., Chen, N., Li, H.: Research on blind equalization algorithm of high-speed visible light communication signal based on machine learning and Marketing. J Commer. Biotechnol. 26, 142–152 (2021). https://doi.org/10.5912/jcb1050

23. Gao, T., Rohm, A.J., Sultan, F., Pagani, M.: Consumers un-tethered: a three-market empirical study of consumers' mobile marketing acceptance. J Bus Res. 66, 2536–2544 (2013). https://doi.org/10.1016/j.jbusres.2013.05.046

24. Gharaibeh, N., Gharaibeh, M.K., Gharaibeh, O., Bdour, W.: Exploring intention to adopt mobile commerce: integrating UTAUT2 with social media. Int. J. Sci. Technol. Res. 9, 3826–3833 (2020)

25. Sultan, F., Rohm, A.J., Gao, T.: Factors influencing consumer acceptance of mobile marketing: a two-country study of youth markets. J. Interact. Mark. 23, 308–320 (2009). https://doi.org/10.1016/j.intmar.2009.07.003

26. Wong, C.H., Tan, G.W.H., Loke, S.P., Ooi, K.B.: Mobile TV: a new form of entertainment? Ind. Manag. Data Syst. 114, 1050–1067 (2014). https://doi.org/10.1108/IMDS-05-2014-0146

27. Shi, J., Zhang, J., Qu, X.: Optimizing distribution strategy for perishable foods using RFiD and sensor technologies. J. Business Indust. Marketing 25, 596–606 (2010). https://doi.org/10.1108/08858621011088338

A Robust Beamforming Algorithm
for Satellite Communication

Ruonan Yang[1], Ying Chen[1]([✉]), Chuili Kong[1], Rong Li[1], Jun Wang[1],
and Kai Wang[2]

[1] Huawei Technologies Co., Ltd., Hangzhou, China
chenying18@huawei.com
[2] PengCheng Laboratory, Shenzhen, China
wangk01@pcl.ac.cn

Abstract. The triangular lattice is preferred in the case when the available estate is limited, since it entails a higher element density than that obtainable with a square lattice of identical inter-element distance. However, the antenna pattern of the triangular lattice is very sensitive to the change of the beam pointing direction due to its nonuniform distribution of beam gain, which probably results in a large SNR decrease with a minor beam pointing error. To address this issue, in this paper, we focus on the two dimensions, i.e., the elevation angle and the azimuth angle, and propose an adaptive azimuth adjustment algorithm to overcome the performance loss caused by the unpredictable elevation angle's variation. Simulation results reveal that the total SNR reduction is less than 0.18dB when the elevation angle changes up to $\pm 5°$, which demonstrates the robustness of our proposed algorithm.

Keywords: Beamforming · Triangular lattice antenna · Satellite communication

1 Introduction

With the breakthrough of satellite manufacturing and launching technologies in recent years, the Low Earth Orbit (LEO) satellite system is widely investigated as a part of the 6G network [1–3]. It not only provides communications with broadband and wide range IoT services around the world, but also brings other new functions such as precision enhanced positioning, navigation, and real time earth observation, with the potential of seamless coverage of the earth in a cost effective way.

For LEO satellite, the link budget is normally limited due to the large propagation loss. Thus, it is natural to use antenna arrays at satellite to provide a directive beam to User Equipment (UE) and, at the same time, suppress the radiation in other directions. Alternatively, the directive beam can be generated by a phased antenna array. To enforce a desired far field pattern, each location and feeding of individual elements in the antenna array is properly selected. Typically, the operative multibeam satellite systems usually employ four color frequency reuse to reduce the interbeam interference (IBI) and multibeam pre-

J. Zhao (Ed.): WiSATS 2023, LNICST 509, pp. 94–105, 2023.
https://doi.org/10.1007/978-3-031-34851-8_8

coding for the same color. In terms of the beam associated way, moving beams and earth-fixed beams are discussed by the 3rd Generation Partnership Project (3GPP). In the moving beam system, the beam directions are unchanged, and hence the beam footprint on earth is moving fast at the same speed level of the satellite. Therefore, even though the position of a UE is fixed, its serving beam is always changing, which causes large signaling overhead by frequent handover and a large Signal-to-Noise Ratio (SNR) change. In contrast, the beam direction always points to the UE in the earth-fixed beam system [4,5], which ensures a reduced handover rate, and low SNR variation. Motivated by this, in this paper, we focus on the earth-fixed beam system.

In most of the planar array layout studied thus far in literature, there are two frequently used cases, namely, square and triangular lattice arrays. The former's antenna elements are deployed on a regular square grid, whereas the latter elements are on a regular triangular grid. Given the same inter-element distance, the triangular lattice entails a higher element density than the counterpart of the square lattice, which indicates a smaller array size [6–10]. Therefore, the triangular lattice is preferred in satellite systems since it at some extent reduces the size and weight of the satellite payload. However, the antenna pattern of the triangular lattice is very sensitive to the change of the beam pointing direction. Possible pointing error may be introduced due to random vibrations or movements of the telescope platform known as jitter, especially for limited size of satellite antenna aperture [11,12]. [13] presented a typical value of jitter in terrestrial system. For satellite communication system, it would be more serious. For example, with a small variation of the elevation angle, i.e., $\pm 5°$, the SNR decreases significantly, i.e., by approximately 2–6 dB. This loss is nontrivial especially for power-limited LEO satellite systems. Motivated by this, in this paper, we present a detailed performance investigation of the satellite system by considering the impact of the jitter. In particular, the main contributions are highlighted as follows:

- We first formulate the association between the Earth Centered Inertial (ECI) coordinate system and the local satellite's antenna system, which ensure that the satellite beams coverage a UE or a specific area on the earth, by taking the rotation of the earth into account.
- Then, we investigate the impact of the azimuth angle on the beam gain loss for a targeted UE when the satellite antenna's jitter occurs. Simulation results demonstrate that the jitter causes the SNR loss of 2–6 dB, which is highly undesirable for the very power-limited LEO satellite systems.
- Fortunately, we find an interesting phenomenon: for a certain target elevation, there is at least one best azimuth direction that can make the beam most tolerant for elevation variation. Based on this, we propose an adaptive azimuth adjustment algorithm to improve the robustness to the variation of elevation angle. Simulation results show that our proposed algorithm can at least guarantee the total SNR decreases no more than 0.18dB when the elevation angle change $\pm 5°$.

The rest of this paper is organized as follows. The system model and problem formulation are presented in Sect. 2. The robust beamforming algorithm is designed in Sect. 3. Simulation results are provided in Sect. 4. The conclusion is remarked in Sect. 5.

Notation: scalars are denoted by lower case italic letters $(a, b, ...)$, vectors by lower case boldface letters $(\mathbf{a}, \mathbf{b}, ...)$, and matrices by boldface capitals $(\mathbf{A}, \mathbf{B}, ...)$. Italic capitals are used to denote index upper bound $(k = 1, ..., K)$. The notation $\|\cdot\|$ denotes the Euclid norm. The cross product of $\mathbf{a}$ and $\mathbf{b}$ is indicated by $\mathbf{a} \times \mathbf{b}$, whereas the dot product is $\mathbf{a} \cdot \mathbf{b}$.

2   System Model

We consider a satellite communication network in the ECI coordinate system. As shown in Fig. 1, the Z-axis is pointed to the earth center, and the X-axis is the velocity vector, and Y-axis can be obtained by the right hand criterion. Therefore, the corresponding unit vectors of X-Y-Z axis can be written as

Fig. 1. Orbit coordinate system of the satellite.

$$\mathbf{r}_Z = -\frac{\mathbf{p}_s}{\|\mathbf{p}_s\|}; \mathbf{r}_X = \frac{\mathbf{v}_s}{\|\mathbf{v}_s\|}; \mathbf{r}_Y = \mathbf{r}_z \times \mathbf{r}_x \qquad (1)$$

where $\mathbf{p}_s$ and $\mathbf{v}_s$ denote the position and velocity vector of the satellite. Thus the unit vector pointed from satellite to a UE located on the earth can be constructed as

$$\rho = \frac{\mathbf{p}_s - \mathbf{p}_u}{\|\mathbf{p}_s - \mathbf{p}_u\|} \qquad (2)$$

where $\mathbf{p}_u$ denotes the position of the UE. Let θ denote the elevation angle between the observed direction and XOY plane, and φ denote the azimuth angle between the projection on XOY plane of the observed direction and X axis. The corresponding elevation angle θ can be calculated as

$$\theta = \arccos \frac{\rho \cdot \mathbf{r}_Z}{\|\rho\| \|\mathbf{r}_Z\|} \qquad (3)$$

Let β denote the angle between the vector ρ and X-axis, we have the following formula

$$\|\rho\|\cos\beta = \|\rho\|\sin\theta\cos\varphi \tag{4}$$

where $\cos\beta$ is calculated as

$$\cos\beta = \frac{\rho \cdot \mathbf{r}_X}{\|\rho\|\|\mathbf{r}_X\|} \tag{5}$$

Therefore, the value of φ can be obtained as

$$\varphi = \arccos\frac{\rho \cdot \mathbf{r}_X}{\|\rho\|\|\mathbf{r}_X\|\sin\theta} \tag{6}$$

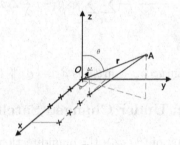

Fig. 2. Antenna coordinate system of a triangular grid array.

Suppose that a triangular grid array antenna with $N_x \times N_y$ elements as illustrated in Fig. 2. To describe the direction of the target UE clearly, let O-xyz denote the antenna coordinate system, the distance difference between the (i,j)-th element and the coordinate origin in space is

$$\triangle L = \frac{\mathbf{d}_{ij} \cdot \mathbf{r}}{\|\mathbf{r}\|} \tag{7}$$

where $\mathbf{d}_{ij}$ denotes the vector from the coordinate origin to the (i,j)-th element, and $\mathbf{r}$ is the unit vector from the coordinate origin to the target. If the antenna array is going to form a beam at (θ_0, φ_0), $\triangle L$ can also be written as

$$\triangle L = \|\mathbf{d}_{ij}\|_x\sin\theta_0\cos\varphi_0 + \|\mathbf{d}_{ij}\|_y\sin\theta_0\sin\varphi_0 \tag{8}$$

where $\|\mathbf{d}_{ij}\|_x$ denotes the length of the projection of $\mathbf{d}_{ij}$ on x axis and $\|\mathbf{d}_{ij}\|_y$ denotes the length of the projection of $\mathbf{d}_{ij}$ on y axis.

Consequently, the phase difference between the (i,j)-th element and the reference element at coordinate origin can be obtained by

$$\phi_{ij} = \frac{2\pi}{\lambda} \cdot (\|\mathbf{d}_{ij}\|_x\sin\theta_0\cos\varphi_0 + \|\mathbf{d}_{ij}\|_y\sin\theta_0\sin\varphi_0) \tag{9}$$

where λ is the wavelength. Then the pattern of the triangular lattice array antenna with $N_x \times N_y$ elements is given by

$$F_{\theta_0,\varphi_0}(\theta,\varphi) = \sum_{i=1}^{N_x} \sum_{j=1}^{N_y} \frac{1}{N_x \times N_y} W \cdot \exp(j\phi_{ij}) \tag{10}$$

where W is the phase excitation for different elements on the direction of θ, φ,

$$W = \exp\left[-j\frac{2\pi}{\lambda} \cdot (\|\mathbf{d}_{ij}\|_x \sin\theta\cos\varphi + \|\mathbf{d}_{ij}\|_y \sin\theta\sin\varphi)\right] \tag{11}$$

To simplify the expression of antenna pattern, $F_{\theta_0,\varphi_0}(\theta,\varphi)$ can be rewritten as

$$F_{\theta_0,\varphi_0}(\theta,\varphi) = \frac{1}{N_x \times N_y} \sum_{i=1}^{N_x} \sum_{j=1}^{N_y} \exp\left[-j\frac{2\pi}{\lambda}\triangle w_{\theta_0,\varphi_0}(\theta,\varphi)\right] \tag{12}$$

where

$$\triangle w_{\theta_0,\varphi_0}(\theta,\varphi) = \|\mathbf{d}_{ij}\|_x (\sin\theta\cos\varphi - \sin\theta_0\cos\varphi_0) + \|\mathbf{d}_{ij}\|_y (\sin\theta\sin\varphi - \sin\theta_0\sin\varphi_0)$$

3   Beam Direction Under Changed Satellite Attitude

For a given beam direction of (θ_0,φ_0), the omnidirectional antenna gain can be obtained by

$$G_{\theta_0,\varphi_0}(\theta,\varphi) = 20\log_{10}\|F_{\theta_0,\varphi_0}(\theta,\varphi)\| \tag{13}$$

where the maximum beam gain $G_t = G_{\theta_0,\varphi_0}(\theta_0,\varphi_0)$ is at the direction of (θ_0,φ_0). When a slight jitter occurs, the maximum beam gain shifts to another direction, e.g., (θ_1,φ_1). Therefore, the real beam gain at the target direction $G_t' = G_{\theta_1,\varphi_1}(\theta_0,\varphi_0)$ becomes

$$G_t' = 20\log_{10}\|\frac{1}{N_x \times N_y}\sum_{i=1}^{N_x}\sum_{j=1}^{N_y}\exp\left[-j\frac{2\pi}{\lambda}\triangle w_{\theta_1,\varphi_1}(\theta_0,\varphi_0)\right]\| \tag{14}$$

The beam gain loss at the target direction $\triangle G_t = G_t - G_t'$ is

$$\triangle G_t = 20\log_{10}\frac{\|\sum_{i=1}^{N_x}\sum_{j=1}^{N_y}\exp\left[-j\frac{2\pi}{\lambda}\triangle w_{\theta_0,\varphi_0}(\theta_0,\varphi_0)\right]\|}{\|\sum_{i=1}^{N_x}\sum_{j=1}^{N_y}\exp\left[-j\frac{2\pi}{\lambda}\triangle w_{\theta_1,\varphi_1}(\theta_0,\varphi_0)\right]\|} \tag{15}$$

Figure 3 shows the beam gain of a triangular grid phased array antenna. Assume that the jitter of satellite only change the value of θ, it can be observed that when the target θ changes, the beam gain loss for different φ is different. For example, in Fig. 3(a), the target UE is at the direction of $(5°, 90°)$, when θ changes to $10°$, the beam gain loss is nearly 3dB; in constant, as shown in Fig. 3(b), the target UE is at the direction of $(5°, 180°)$, when θ varies the same level, the beam gain loss is only 0.1dB. The aforementioned interesting phenomenon reveals that, there is always a best φ to make the beam most tolerant

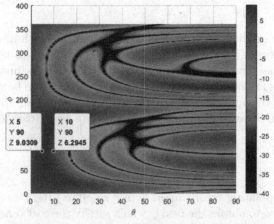

(a) The target beam direction is $(\theta, \varphi) = (5°, 90°)$

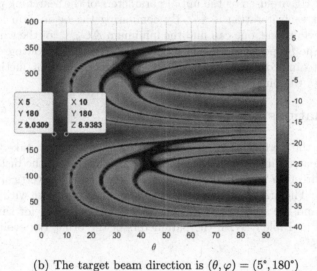

(b) The target beam direction is $(\theta, \varphi) = (5°, 180°)$

Fig. 3. Beam gain of a triangular grid array antenna with different direction.

for the variation of θ. Besides, satellite may change its attitude to enable the solar panel absorb more light energy. That leads to the antenna coordinate system not same as the orbit coordinate system. To describe the real-time attitude of the satellite, a local coordinate system should be established, and the two angles θ and φ should be calculated based on the local coordinate system. Moreover, three angles named the rolling angle α_x, the pitching angle α_y and the course angle α_z are used to describe the Euler angles between the local coordinate system and the orbit coordinate system. Normally, α_y and α_x are very small and the impact is negligible. In the following, we only consider α_z, and have

$$\varphi = \varphi_0 - \alpha_z \tag{16}$$

where φ_0 is the original azimuth and φ is the real azimuth after rotation. For satellite, the jitter is a random variable so that it is hard to know the exactly variation of θ, based on (16), one can obtain the best φ by adjusting the attitude of the satellite, so that the tolerant for the variation of θ can be guaranteed. The target is to find the optimal φ which can make the beam gain difference as little as possible when θ varies. So the cost function can be written as

$$\min_{\varphi} \{\triangle G_{\theta_1,\varphi}\} \tag{17}$$

where $\triangle G_{\theta_1,\varphi} = G_{\theta_1,\varphi}(\theta_1,\varphi) - G_{\theta_1,\varphi}(\theta_0,\varphi)$, where $\theta_1 = \theta_0 + \triangle\theta$, and $\triangle\theta$ is the elevation angle pointing error caused by the satellite jitter.

Consequently, to obtain the best φ which satisfy the cost function, a traversal method can be used. Set N as the number of iterations, the direction (θ_0,φ_0) of the targeted UE are used as the initial parameters of the searching process. The step of θ for each iteration is $\frac{360}{N}$. By comparing the beam gain loss $\triangle G_{\theta_1,\varphi_i}$ with the previous one, one can find the minimum $\triangle G_{\theta_1,\varphi_i}$ of the whole N times iterations. The proposed algorithm is summarized as the following Algorithm 4. Note that, to improve the search speed, some more efficient methods can be adopted, e.g., the binary search algorithm.

4 Simulations and Analysis

To evaluate the performance of the proposed algorithm, we take 4×2 triangular lattice array into consideration. As Fig. 4 illustrated, the distance on the horizontal direction is $dx = 20$ mm and the distance on the vertical direction is $dy = 8.7$ mm. The array antenna is equipped on a LEO satellite with orbit height of 500 km, and the six Keplerian elements of the orbit used for simulation are summarized in Table 1. With the parameters of the orbit, the orbital period is about 5690 s.

Algorithm 1. Optimal azimuth computation

Input: θ_0, φ_0, $\triangle\theta$, N.
Output: φ
1: initial $\varphi = \varphi_0$, $\theta_1 = \theta_0 + \triangle\theta$, $\triangle G_{\theta_1,\varphi_0} = G_{\theta_1,\varphi_0}(\theta_1,\varphi_0) - G_{\theta_1,\varphi_0}(\theta_0,\varphi_0)$,
2: **for** $i = 1$ to $N-1$ **do**
3:    Compute $\varphi_i = (\varphi_0 + i \cdot \frac{360}{N})$;
4:    Compute G_{θ_1,φ_i} with beam direction of (θ_1,φ_i);
5:    Compute beam gain difference $\triangle G_{\theta_1,\varphi_i} = G_{\theta_1,\varphi_i}(\theta_1,\varphi_i) - G_{\theta_1,\varphi_i}(\theta_0,\varphi_i)$.
6:    **if** $\triangle G_{\theta_1,\varphi_i} < \triangle G_{\theta_1,\varphi_0}$ **then**
7:       $\triangle G_{\theta_1,\varphi_0} = \triangle G_{\theta_1,\varphi_i}$
8:       $\varphi = \varphi_i$
9:    **end if**
10: **end for**

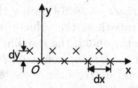

Fig. 4. Layout of 4×2 triangular grid array antenna.

Table 1. Parameters of the LEO orbit.

Eccentricity (e)	0
Semimajor axis (a)	6875800 m
Inclination (i)	$2°$
Longitude of the ascending node (Ω)	$105.98°$
Argument of periapsis (ω)	$72°$
mean anomaly (M)	0

For a target UE, the carrier to noise ratio (CNR) defined in [11] is adopted in order to evaluate the SNR at UE:

$$\text{SNR} = P_t + G(\theta, \varphi) + G/T - k - PL_{fs} - PL_{polar} - PL_{other} - 10\log_{10}(B) \quad (18)$$

where P_t, $G(\theta, \phi)$, G/T, k, B are the satellite transmit power, beam gain, antenna-gain-to noise-temperature, the Boltzmann constant, and the bandwidth, respectively. And the values used for simulation are shown in Table 2. Besides, PL_{fs}, PL_{polar} and PL_{other} are the path losses defined in [14].

Table 2. Simulation Parameters.

Satellite transmit power P_t	11 dBW
Antenna-gain-to noise-temperature G/T	19 dB/K
Boltzmann constant k	–228.6 dBW/K/Hz
Bandwidth B	200 MHz

In the simulation, we assume $\triangle\theta = \pm5°$ and the number of iterations is $N = 360$. To evaluate the proposed algorithm, we use the SNR decrease as a metric to evaluate the performance loss caused by the jitter.

4.1 Nadir Point UE

In this subsection, we focus on the nadir point UE which is the intersection of the Earth center and the satellite's connection on the earth surface. Take the nadir point of observation time $t = 2846\,s$ during the movement of satellite as the target UE position. At this time, the value of θ equals to zero. To ensure the minimum demodulation threshold, the dwelling time of satellite is defined as the time duration when $\theta < 53°$, i.e., from $t = 2744\,s$ to $t = 2946\,s$, as shown in Fig. 5. The value of θ would decrease as the satellite approaches to the UE and vice versa. In the dewelling time, the change of φ is very interesting: It can be seen that under the simulation assumption, φ keeps 360° when the satellite moves towards the UE, i.e., from 2744 s to 2845 s and φ keeps 180° when the satellite moves away from the UE, i.e., from 2846 s to 2946 s.

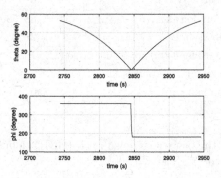

Fig. 5. Elevation and azimuth of the nadir point UE.

By employing the proposed algorithm, the value of original φ and the adjusted φ was shown in Fig. 6. Also, the corresponding total gain decrease with $\pm5°$ shift of elevation angle is presented. In Fig. 6, it presents that during the serving time, the beam gain performance decreases at least 2dB when θ changes $\pm5°$. And the performance loss is as high as almost 6dB when satellite moves upon the target UE. That means with a fixed θ, the beam gain performance is always sensitive to the variation of θ no matter φ is 180° or 360°. Fortunately, this detrimental effect can be mitigated by our proposed algorithm. As can be seen, by updating the value of φ, even if the θ changes $\pm5°$ due to the jitter of satellite, the SNR loss reduces to no more than 0.18dB, which indicates that the proposed algorithm is robust for the θ error. Although the adjusted φ hops frequently between 90° and 270° during the dwelling time, it does not increase the complexity of satellite. This is because, the difference of the SNR loss between the two values is negligible due to the symmetrical character of antenna pattern. Thus, the optimal φ can be either of them without any angle switching, and besides, the computation can be done offline.

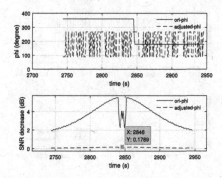

Fig. 6. Performance of the adjusted azimuth for the nadir point UE.

4.2 Non-nadir Point UE

In this subsection, we focus on the non-nadir point UE which is 500 km far away from the nadir point of observation time $t = 2846\,s$ as the UE position. As shown in Fig. 7, the azimuth angle φ varies from about $45°$ to $135°$. The performance of the proposed algorithm is illustrated in Fig. 8. It can be seen that the azimuth angle φ is almost equals to the optimal φ when the satellite moves upon the target UE, so the SNR decrease of the real φ and the adjusted φ is almost the same. Simliar to the case of nadir point UE, the proposed algorithm can always obtain lower SNR decrease during the satellite dwelling time.

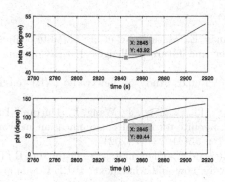

Fig. 7. Elevation and azimuth of the non-nadir point UE.

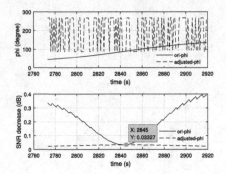

Fig. 8. Performance of the adjusted azimuth for the non-nadir point UE.

5   Conclusion

For triangular grid array, the antenna jitter may cause the difference of the real elevation angle and expected elevation angle, which leads to SNR loss of the target UE. To solve the problem, an adaptive azimuth adjustment algorithm is proposed. By carefully adjust the azimuth angle to the optimal direction, the SNR loss caused by the jitter is minimized and becomes negligible. Then the obtained optimal azimuth angle can be realized by changing the attitude of the satellite. Simulation results show the effectiveness of the proposed algorithm.

References

1. Kodheli, O., Lagunas, E., Maturo, N., et al.: Satellite communications in the new space era: a survey and future challenges. IEEE Commun. Surv. Tutorials **23**, 70–109 (2020)
2. 3GPP TR 38.811 V15.0.0. Study on new radio (NR) to support non-terrestrial networks
3. Liu, X., Lam, K.-Y., Li, F., Zhao, J., Wang, L., Durrani, T.S.: Spectrum sharing for 6G integrated satellite-terrestrial communication networks based on NOMA and CR. IEEE Netw. **35**(4), 28–34 (2021)
4. Shankar, B., Lagunas, M.E., Chatzinotas, S., Ottersten, B.: Precoding for satellite communications: why, how and what next? IEEE Commun. Lett. **25**, 2453–2457 (2021)
5. You, L., Li, K.-X., Wang, J., Gao, X., Xia, X.-G., Ottersten, B.: Massive MIMO transmission for LEO satellite communications. IEEE J. Selected Areas Commun. **38**(8), 1851–1865 (2020)
6. Moon, S., Yun, S., Yom, I., Lee, H.L.: Phased array shaped-beam satellite antenna with boosted-beam control. IEEE Trans. Antennas Propagation **67**(12), 7633–7636 (2019)
7. Kuhlmann, K., Jacob, A.F.: Antenna arrays on rectangular and triangular grids for polarization multiplexing - a comparative study. In: German Microwave Conference 2009, pp. 1–4 (2009)

8. Yun, Y., Jianshu, C., Jianchun, M.: Directional pattern modeling and simulation of triangular grid circular planar array antennas. In: 2010 2nd International Conference on Signal Processing Systems, pp. 666–669 (2010)
9. Rana, B., Lee, I.-G., Hong, I.-P.: Digitally reconfigurable transmitarray with beam-steering and polarization switching capabilities. IEEE Access **9**, 144140–144148 (2021)
10. Rahmat-Samii, Y., Densmore, A.C.: Technology trends and challenges of antennas for satellite communication systems. IEEE Trans. Antennas Propagation **63**(4), 1191–1204 (2015)
11. Toyoshima, M., Jono, T., Nakagawa, K., Yamamoto, A.: Optimum divergence angle of a Gaussian beam wave in the presence of random jitter in free-space laser communication systems. JOSAA **19**(3), 567–571 (2002)
12. Phelps, E., Primmerman, C.A.: Blind compensation of angle jitter for satellite-based ground-imaging lidar. IEEE Trans. Geosci. Remote Sens. **58**(2), 1436–1449 (2020)
13. Kim, I.I., Stieger, R., Koontz, J.A., Moursund, C., Barclay, M., et al.: Wireless optical transmission of fast ethernet, FDDI, ATM, and ESCON protocol data using the TerraLink laser communication system. Optical Eng. **37**, 3143–3155 (1998)
14. 3GPP TR 38.821 V16.0.0. Solutions for NR to support non-terrestrial networks (NTN)

Network Efficiency and Reliability

Average Age of Incorrect Information in Random Access Channels for IoT Systems

Xinye Shao$^{(\boxtimes)}$, Mingchuan Yang, and Qing Guo

Harbin Institute of Technology, Harbin, China
xinyeshaohit@gmail.com, {mcyang,qguo}@hit.edu.cn

Abstract. Age of incorrect information (AoII) has been proposed recently to overcome the shortcomings of age of information (AoI) in internet of things (IoT) systems. AoII takes into account the content of the information by penalizing the sink only when it has an incorrect perception of the monitored source. This is of paramount importance for scenarios where actuations are taken based on the current data sample. On the other hand, random access (RA) has been identified as a promising solution for supporting next-generation IoT systems. Therefore, a thorough understanding of the behaviors of RA policies from the perspective of AoII is key for the design of IoT systems. In this paper, we study two representative RA schemes, namely slotted ALOHA (SA) and irregular repetition slotted ALOHA (IRSA), with Markov sources. We track the AoII evolution for both schemes through a Markovian analysis, where state transition probabilities are derived and closed form expressions for the average AoII are obtained. Simulation results are provided to validate our analysis. The study reveals the influences of the Markov source on the system performance as well as the design trade-offs for IRSA. Furthermore, the performance of SA and IRSA are compared under various settings, showing the cases where IRSA can largely outperform SA in terms of average AoII.

Keywords: Age of incorrect information · Random access · Slotted ALOHA · Irregular repetition slotted ALOHA · IoT

1 Introduction

As a key component of the next-generation wireless communication network, internet of things (IoT) has served as a rich source of research problems at all protocol layers. In particular, massive machine type communications (mMTC) are characterized by a very large number of terminals sporadically communicating to a central gateway over a shared wireless channel in an unpredictable fashion. In this situation, at the link layer, traditional grant-based access policies

This research was funded by the National Natural Science Foundation of China under grant numbers 62071146 and 62171151 and the Fundamental Research Funds for the Central Universities (No. HIT.OCEF. 2021012).

J. Zhao (Ed.): WiSATS 2023, LNICST 509, pp. 109–129, 2023.
https://doi.org/10.1007/978-3-031-34851-8_9

become especially inefficient due to the high signaling overhead as well as the high complexity of coordination. Random access (RA) schemes, thanks to their grant-free nature and simplicity, have attracted more attention. Several IoT commercial solutions and standards (e.g., NB-IoT [19], SigFox [18], LoRa [8], etc.) are based on the simple ALOHA protocol and its variations.

In RA, packets transmitted by different terminals may collide with each other, which has limited the number of terminals that can be supported. Irregular repetition slotted ALOHA (IRSA) proposed in [7] represents one of the most appealing solutions to overcome packet collisions. The basic idea of IRSA is to transmit multiple packet replicas at the transmitter side within a frame consisting of slots and employ successive interference cancellation (SIC) at the receiver side to resolve packet collisions. The throughput of IRSA has been shown to be comparable to that of grant-based schemes. Due to its potential, the ETSI DVB-RCS2 standard has included IRSA as the link layer protocol for return-link satellite communications [4] and IRSA variations [14,17] have been developed, which further improve the performance of IRSA.

On the other hand, many IoT applications (e.g., environmental monitoring, industrial automation, etc.) see the need to have a best real-time estimation of the remote process monitored by each terminal. In these cases, a fresh view of each terminal at the gateway is critical for correct and efficient decision making. Traditional metrics (e.g., throughput, delay, packet loss rate (PLR)) commonly used for designing RA schemes cannot well capture the notion of information freshness and age of information (AoI) [5] has emerged as a pioneering metric to overcome the shortcomings of traditional metrics. AoI is defined as the time elapsed since the generation time stamp of the last received packet at the receiver. Triggered by this novel concept, existing RA schemes designed based on traditional metrics have been revisited and redesigned.

The formula for the average AoI (AAoI) of slotted ALOHA (SA) was first derived in [20], which was then extended to pure ALOHA in [21]. It was revealed that the AAoI of SA and the system throughput are inversely proportional. To break this limitation, a threshold-based SA policy relying on the feedback from the receiver was proposed in [2], where terminals keep silent before their ages reach a fixed age threshold. The age performance of this policy was later analyzed in [22], showing a significant improvement over SA. In parallel, the first analysis of AoI for IRSA was presented in [11] and [10], providing a powerful tool for designing age-optimal IRSA schemes. It was demonstrated that IRSA exhibits a remarkable potential in terms of AoI compared to the SA strategy. Another independent analysis and optimization of AoI for IRSA was reported in [15] with different settings on the packet generation model and the SIC process. Leaning on the results in [10], the optimization of IRSA with heterogeneous terminals requiring different levels of AoI was performed in [13].

Although AoI has been widely deemed as a fundamental metric for communication systems, it has some intrinsic limitations. That the value of AoI increases linearly with time may become unreliable for quantifying the effect of stale information. In view of this, a more general age penalty function following a power law of the time elapsed has been investigated for SA in Gilbert-Elliot channels in [12]. Another important limitation is that AoI does not account for the information content of the update packets nor the current knowledge at the receiver. For instance, the age penalty keeps growing even when the receiver has perfect knowledge of the monitored process. To remedy this, a new metric called age of incorrect information (AoII) has been proposed in [9]. AoII is defined as the time elapsed since the receiver has an incorrect perception of the monitored process. Therefore, AoII measures the staleness of the information content rather than of the time stamps. Motivated by this, a recent work [6] studied the problem of scheduling multiple terminals, each monitoring a Markov process, with the aim to minimize the mean AoII.

To the best of our knowledge, AoII has not been explored for RA schemes. Since RA is of great significance for supporting mMTC, it is necessary to look at RA schemes from an AoII viewpoint. In this paper, we provide the first study of the AoII metric for SA and IRSA with Markov sources. Specifically, closed form expressions of average AoII are derived for SA and IRSA. Based on this, the influences of Markov sources on the average AoII performance are analyzed. Our results reveal in what cases IRSA can largely outperform SA and how the optimal operating frame length of IRSA heavily depends on the nature of Markov sources being tracked. The analytical results can be readily used as an efficient tool for determining optimal system operating parameters, which is important for deploying RA schemes for mMTC.

The rest of the paper is organized as follows. Section 2 introduces the system model and some preliminaries. Then, derivations of average AoII for IRSA and SA are provided in Sect. 3. Simulation results are presented and discussed in Sect. 4. Finally, Sect. 5 concludes the paper.

2   System Model and Preliminaries

2.1   Network Model

We focus on a communication system where N_u terminals, each equipped with sensors, monitor processes of interest and send update packets over a shared wireless channel to a central gateway using RA strategies. The gateway updates estimations of these remote processes based on the last received packets. The aim of the communication system is to have the best real-time estimation of the process at each terminal.

Time is divided into slots of same duration, each fitting one packet transmission and all terminals are synchronized to this pattern. In the rest of this paper, we consider time to be discrete and normalized to the slot duration.

More concretely, terminal i observes a discrete-time random process $(X_i(t))_{t \in \mathbb{N}}$ and the gateway maintains an estimation of the process, denoted by $(\hat{X}_i(t))_{t \in \mathbb{N}}$. Packets are generated by sampling the process and delivered to the gateway over a RA channel with delay D. Denote $I_i(t)$ as the indicator for packet reception such that $I_i(t) = 1$ if an update packet from terminal i is successfully decoded at time

t and $I_i(t) = 0$ otherwise. Assume that the sampling time is negligible compared to the transmission delay. Then, the estimation process is updated by the gateway following

$$\hat{X}_i(t) = \begin{cases} X_i(t-D) \ I_i(t) = 1 \\ \hat{X}_i(t-1) \ I_i(t) = 0. \end{cases} \tag{1}$$

It is important to observe that the information brought by the update packet is not real-time due to the time delay. And the estimation process keeps its value when no packet is successfully decoded.

The random process $(X_i(t))_{t \in \mathbb{N}}$ monitored by terminal i is considered to be a discrete-time Markov chain with N_s states $\{S_1, \ldots, S_{N_s}\}$. The one-step transition probabilities are given by

$$p_s(j,k) = P(X_i(t+1) = S_k \mid X_i(t) = S_j)$$
$$= \begin{cases} p_R \ j = k \\ p_t \ j \neq k, \end{cases} \tag{2}$$

where $0 < p_R < 1$ denotes the probability of remaining at the same state and $0 < p_t < 1$ the probability of transitioning to another state. It follows immediately that

$$p_R + (N_s - 1)p_t = 1. \tag{3}$$

We assume that processes at different terminals are independent of each other.

Next, we define two quantities regarding this Markov chain, which will be useful in Set. III and IV. Without risk of confusion, we drop the terminal index i. Let T_t denote the first passage time from state S_j to S_k ($j \neq k$), i.e., $T_t = \min\{n \geq 2 \text{ such that } X(n) = S_k \mid X(1) = S_j\} - 1$. Using the method in [3, Section 7.4], the expectation of T_t can be obtained as

$$\overline{T_t} = \frac{1}{p_t}. \tag{4}$$

Note that $\overline{T_t}$ can also be interpreted as the mean time it takes for the Markov chain to transit back to the same state after it leaves the state.

Let T_R be the time duration of staying at the same state. Then, its expectation can be readily calculated as

$$\overline{T_R} = \sum_{k=0}^{\infty} k p_R^k (1 - p_R) + 1 = \frac{1}{1 - p_R}. \tag{5}$$

2.2   Random Access Schemes

As for RA strategies, SA and IRSA are considered for transmitting update packets. The simple collision model is adopted for packet reception, i.e., packets in collisions are considered to be lost and packets without collisions are always successfully decoded. For both schemes, no feedback nor retransmissions are considered.

Slotted ALOHA (SA). In SA, each terminal becomes active independently at each slot with probability μ. Each active terminal samples its process of interest at the start of the slot and transmits an update packet to the gateway. Each packet transmission consumes one slot, thus delay $D = 1$.

The channel load, defined as the average number of active terminals per slot, is

$$G_{sa} = N_u \mu.$$

Denote PLR_{sa} as the probability for a packet to be lost in SA. Based on the collision model, a packet can be successfully decoded when no other terminals are active at the same slot. Therefore, $PLR_{sa} = 1 - (1 - \mu)^{(N_u - 1)}$. Then, the throughput of SA, defined as the average number of successfully decoded packets per slot, can be obtained as

$$S_{sa} = G_{sa}(1 - PLR_{sa}) = N_u \mu (1 - \mu)^{(N_u - 1)}. \tag{6}$$

Irregular Repetition Slotted ALOHA (IRSA) [7]. In IRSA, slots are organized into frames, each consisting of m slots. Each terminal becomes active at each frame independently with probability ρ. Each active terminal samples its process of interest at the start of the frame and generates an update packet. Then, r replicas of this packet are created with probability $\Lambda(r)$ and these replicas are transmitted at r slots uniformly selected within the frame. The degree distribution of IRSA is defined as

$$\Lambda(x) = \sum_{r=1}^{r_m} \Lambda(r)x^r,$$

where r_m denotes the maximum number of replicas. Similarly to SA, the channel load for IRSA is defined as

$$G_{irsa} = N_u \rho / m.$$

At the gateway, after a whole frame is received, the SIC process is performed to decode packets. We assume that the time of executing the SIC process is negligible in comparison with the frame length. Then, due to the frame structure, each packet in IRSA is decoded with delay $D = m$. Denoting the probability for a packet in IRSA not to be successfully decoded as PLR_{irsa}, the throughput of IRSA can be expressed as

$$S_{irsa} = G_{irsa}(1 - \text{PLR}_{irsa}) = \frac{N_u \rho}{m}(1 - \text{PLR}_{irsa}). \tag{7}$$

The calculation of PLR_{irsa} is known to be difficult, for which no exact closed form expressions exist in the literature. In this paper, we adopt the method introduced in [10], which combines the results from [1] and [16] and achieves good approximations for calculating PLR_{irsa}. Specifically, PLR_{irsa} is calculated as

$$\text{PLR}_{irsa} = P_{wf}(G_{irsa}, \Lambda(x)) + P_{ef}(G_{irsa}, \Lambda(x)), \tag{8}$$

where P_{wf} and P_{ef} represent the PLR of IRSA in the waterfall and error-floor region respectively. The expressions for these two functions can be found in [1] and [16] respectively.

2.3 Age of Incorrect Informaiton (AoII) [9]

The gateway relies on estimation $\hat{X}_i(t)$ to make decisions or drive feedback loops. Therefore, the gateway should be increasingly penalized when staying in an erroneous state ($\hat{X}_i(t) \neq X_i(t)$) and not penalized when having perfect knowledge of the monitored process. The metric AoII well captures this notion. Mathematically, AoII for terminal i at time t is defined as [9]

$$\Delta_i(t) = (t - V_i(t))\mathbb{1}\{\hat{X}_i(t) \neq X_i(t)\}, \tag{9}$$

where $\mathbb{1}\{.\}$ is the indicator function and

$$V_i(t) = \max\{t_0 < t \text{ such that } \hat{X}_i(t_0) = X_i(t_0)\}$$

denotes the last time instant where the estimation is correct. An example of AoII evolution with $N_s = 3$ according to (9) is provided in Fig. 1. At slot 1, 2 and 5, the gateway has perfect estimation of the process, leading to zero penalty. In contrast, AoII increases at slot 3 and 4, resulting from the erroneous estimation of the process.

$\hat{X}_i(t)$	S_2	S_2	S_2	S_2	S_1
$X_i(t)$	S_2	S_2	S_3	S_1	S_1
$\Delta_i(t)$	0	0	1	2	0
	slot 1	slot 2	slot 3	slot 4	slot 5

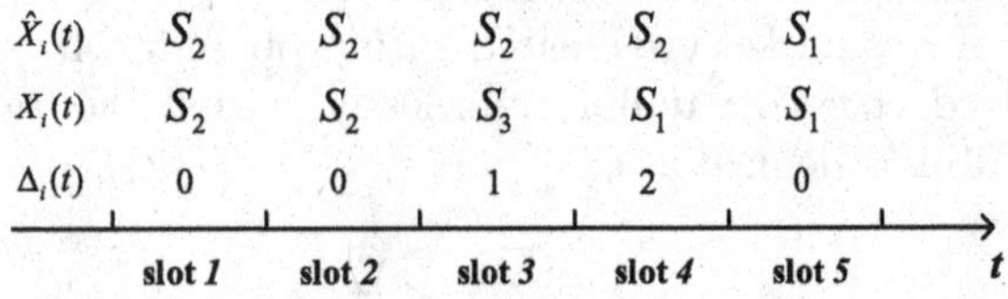

Fig. 1. An example of AoII evolution with $N_s = 3$.

In this paper, we are interested in the average AoII

$$\overline{\Delta} = \frac{1}{N_u} \sum_{i=1}^{N_u} \overline{\Delta}_i, \tag{10}$$

where $\overline{\Delta}_i$ is the average AoII of terminal i, which is defined as

$$\overline{\Delta}_i = \lim_{T \to \infty} \frac{1}{T} \sum_{t=1}^{T} \Delta_i(t). \tag{11}$$

3 Derivations of Average AoII for SA and IRSA

In this section, we derive the expressions of average AoII for SA and IRSA by means of a Markovian analysis similar to that in [10]. Note that all terminals in the system operate independently of each other, thus

$$\overline{\Delta} = \frac{1}{N_u} \sum_{i=1}^{N_u} \overline{\Delta}_i = \overline{\Delta}_i. \tag{12}$$

Based on this, in the following, we concentrate on the evolution of $\Delta_i(t)$ for a generic terminal i.

From (9) and Fig. 1, we can observe that the value of AoII at next slot will either increase by 1 if the gateway stays in an erroneous state or be reset to 0 if the gateway has a correct estimation, which can be expressed as

$$\Delta_i(t+1) = \begin{cases} \Delta_i(t) + 1 & \hat{X}_i(t+1) \neq X_i(t+1) \\ 0 & \hat{X}_i(t+1) = X_i(t+1). \end{cases} \tag{13}$$

The random process $X_i(t)$ is characterized by the Markov chain introduced in Sect. 2, while the estimation process $\hat{X}_i(t)$ is related to the RA scheme. We first analyze the case of SA.

3.1 Slotted ALOHA Average AoII

Recall that in SA, each packet transmission consumes one slot, i.e., $D = 1$. According to (1), $\hat{X}_i(t+1)$ is obtained as

$$\hat{X}_i(t+1) = \begin{cases} X_i(t) & I_i(t+1) = 1 \\ \hat{X}_i(t) & I_i(t+1) = 0. \end{cases} \tag{14}$$

Leaning on this and noticing that all terminals operate independently over successive slots, the stochastic process $(\Delta_i(t))_{t\in\mathbb{N}}$ in SA is therefore Markovian and can be fully characterized by a discrete-time Markov chain with state space $\mathbb{N}_0$. Next, we derive one-step transition probabilities

$$p_{sa}(j, k) = P(\Delta_i(t+1) = k \mid \Delta_i(t) = j), \quad j, k \in \mathbb{N}_0 \tag{15}$$

describing this Markov chain by considering two cases:

$\Delta_i(t) = 0$. In this case, the gateway has perfect knowledge of the remote process at current slot, i.e., $\hat{X}_i(t) = X_i(t)$. According to (14), the estimation at next slot will be updated as $\hat{X}_i(t+1) = X_i(t)$. By (13), $\Delta_i(t+1)$ will equal 0 if the remote process remains at its current state at next slot, which happens with probability p_R; $\Delta_i(t+1)$ will equal 1 if the remote process leaves its current state, which occurs with probability $1 - p_R$.

$\Delta_i(t) \neq 0$. In this case, the gateway has an incorrect perception of the remote process at current slot, i.e., $\hat{X}_i(t) \neq X_i(t)$. According to (14), the estimation at next slot depends on the packet reception result. Specifically, $\hat{X}_i(t+1) = X_i(t)$ if terminal i generates a packet and the packet is received with no collisions. This event happens with probability $\mu(1 - PLR_{sa}) = S_{sa}/N_u$. In this situation, $\Delta_i(t+1)$ will equal 0 if the remote process remains at its current state, which happens with probability p_R and $\Delta_i(t)+1$ if the remote process leaves its current state, which occurs with probability $1 - p_R$.

On the other hand, if no packet is successfully decoded, then $\hat{X}_i(t+1) = \hat{X}_i(t) \neq X_i(t)$. In this situation, $\Delta_i(t+1)$ will equal 0 if the remote process transits to state $\hat{X}_i(t)$, which happens with probability p_t and $\Delta_i(t) + 1$ if the process remains at its current state or transits to other $N_s - 2$ states, which occurs with probability $1 - p_t$.

We summarize above results by expressing (15) as follows:

$$p_{sa}(j,k) = \begin{cases} p_R & j = 0, k = 0 \\ S_{sa}/N_u p_R + (1 - S_{sa}/N_u)p_t & j \neq 0, k = 0 \\ 1 - p_{sa}(j,0) & k = j+1 \\ 0 & \text{otherwise.} \end{cases} \tag{16}$$

Leaning on (16), we are able to track AoII for SA at any time given the initial AoII. Nevertheless, we are interested in the long-term average AoII, for which a closed-from expression is provided as follows:

Proposition 1. *The average AoII of a SA system monitoring remote Markov processes of Sect. 2, measured in slots, is given by*

$$\overline{\Delta}_{sa} = \frac{1 - p_R}{\alpha(\alpha + 1 - p_R)}, \tag{17}$$

where $\alpha = S_{sa}/N_u p_R + (1 - S_{sa}/N_u)p_t$.

Proof. We first show that the Markov chain characterizing the stochastic process $(\Delta_i(t))_{t \in \mathbb{N}}$ of SA is irreducible, which requires that there exist $n > 0$ such that the n-step transition probability between any state-pair (j, k) is strictly positive. Based on (16), we can observe that for $k > j$, the transition from j to k can take place in $k - j$ steps with probability $(1 - \alpha)^{k-j} > 0$ if $j \neq 0$ and $(1 - p_R)(1 - \alpha)^{k-j-1} > 0$ if $j = 0$. Otherwise, the transition can occur by first moving to state 0 in one step and then to state k in k steps. This event happens with probability $\alpha(1 - p_R)(1 - \alpha)^{k-1} > 0$ if $j \neq 0$ and $p_R > 0$ if $j = 0$. Therefore, the statement of irreducibility holds. From (16), we can also observe that state 0 has period 1, indicating that the chain is aperiodic. Since the chain is irreducible and aperiodic, steady-state probabilities $\{\pi_k\}$, $k \in \mathbb{N}_0$ exist and can be obtained by solving the balance equations:

$$\begin{cases} \pi_k = \pi_0 p_R + \sum_{k=1}^{\infty} \pi_k \alpha \overset{(a)}{=} \pi_0 p_R + (1 - \pi_0)\alpha & k = 0 \\ \pi_k = \pi_0(1 - p_R)(1 - \alpha)^{k-1} & k > 0 \end{cases} \tag{18}$$

where (a) is due to the normalization equation $\sum_{k=0}^{\infty} \pi_k = 1$. For $k = 0$, we can readily compute π_k from the first equation in (18) as

$$\pi_0 = \frac{\alpha}{1 + \alpha - p_R}. \tag{19}$$

Otherwise π_k can be obtained directly by substituting (19) into the second equation in (18).

It can be concluded that the process $(\Delta_i(t))_{t \in \mathbb{N}}$ is ergodic because it has positive steady-state probabilities. Based on this ergodicity, we have

$$
\begin{aligned}
\overline{\Delta}_{sa} &= \lim_{T \to \infty} \frac{1}{T} \sum_{t=1}^{T} \Delta_i(t) = \sum_{k=0}^{\infty} \pi_k k \\
&= \sum_{k=1}^{\infty} \frac{\alpha}{1 + \alpha - p_R} (1 - p_R)(1 - \alpha)^{k-1} k \\
&= \frac{1 - p_R}{\alpha(\alpha + 1 - p_R)}
\end{aligned}
\tag{20}
$$

concluding the proof.   □

3.2   IRSA Average AoII

Recall that in IRSA, due to the frame structure, each update packet is decoded with delay $D = m$. By (1), the estimation process in IRSA should be updated as

$$
\hat{X}_i(t) = \begin{cases} X_i(t - m) & I_i(t) = 1 \\ \hat{X}_i(t - 1) & I_i(t) = 0. \end{cases}
\tag{21}
$$

Without loss of generality, we start tracking the AoII process of IRSA at the beginning of a generic frame by setting $t = 1$ at the first slot of the frame. According to the IRSA protocol, the SIC decoding process starts after a whole frame is received. In other words, packets transmitted at current frame are decoded at the start of the next frame. Therefore, in IRSA, the estimation process can only be updated at time

$$
t \in \Phi = \{t_l = (l - 1)m + 1, l \in \mathbb{N}\},
$$

i.e., at the first slot of each frame. No packets are decoded at other time, i.e., $I_i(t) = 0$ at time $t \notin \Phi$. Based on this observation, we divide time into two sets: $t \in \Phi$ and $t \notin \Phi$. According to (21), the estimation process at $t \notin \Phi$ keeps its value

$$
\hat{X}_i(t_l + k) = \hat{X}_i(t_l), \quad k \in \{1, \ldots, m - 1\}
\tag{22}
$$

and the estimation process at $t \in \Phi$ is updated as

$$
\hat{X}_i(t_{l+1}) = \begin{cases} X_i(t_l) & I_i(t_{l+1}) = 1 \\ \hat{X}_i(t_{l+1} - 1) & I_i(t_{l+1}) = 0 \end{cases}
\tag{23}
$$

Now let us focus on the evolution of $\Delta_i(t)$. Denote $T_l = \{t_l, \ldots, t_{l+1} - 1\}$ as the set of time indexes within the l-th frame. By (13) and (22), we can see that the random process $(\Delta_i(t))_{t \in T_l}$ within frame l is Markovian. It can be characterized by a discrete-time Markov chain with initial state $\Delta_i(t_l)$ and state space $\mathbb{N}_0$. The one-step state transition probabilities

$$
q_{irsa}(j, k) = P(\Delta_i(t + 1) = k \mid \Delta_i(t) = j), \quad j, k \in \mathbb{N}_0
\tag{24}
$$

for this chain can be derived by following similar steps in SA except that no packet reception needs to be considered. Therefore, we have

$$q_{irsa}(j,k) = \begin{cases} p_R & j = 0, k = 0 \\ p_t & j \neq 0, k = 0 \\ 1 - q_{irsa}(j,0) & k = j+1 \\ 0 & \text{otherwise}. \end{cases} \quad (25)$$

Next, we concentrate on AoII at the first slot of each frame, i.e., the random process $(\Delta_i(t))_{t \in \Phi}$, where the packet can be decoded and then the estimation process is updated. Since each terminal operates independently over successive frame in IRSA, $(\Delta_i(t))_{t \in \Phi}$ is also Markovian, which can be described by a discrete-time Markov chain with state space $\mathbb{N}_0$. The one-step transition probabilities

$$p_{irsa}(j,k) = P(\Delta_i(t_{l+1}) = k \mid \Delta_i(t_l) = j), \quad j, k \in \mathbb{N}_0 \quad (26)$$

can be obtained by considering two cases similar to that in SA, however, with important differences:

$\Delta_i(t_l) = 0$. In this case, $\hat{X}_i(t_l) = X_i(t_l)$. According to (23), $\hat{X}_i(t_{l+1})$ will be updated as $X_i(t_l)$ regardless of the packet reception result at time t_{l+1}. Therefore, $\Delta_i(t_{l+1})$ can be viewed as the state at the m-th step for the Markov chain described by (25) given initial state $\Delta_i(t_l) = 0$. Thus we have

$$P(\Delta_i(t_{l+1}) = k \mid \Delta_i(t_l) = 0) = q_{irsa}^{(m)}(0,k), k \in \{0, \ldots, m\}, \quad (27)$$

where $q_{irsa}^{(m)}$ denotes the m-step transition probability.

$\Delta_i(t_l) \neq 0$. In this case, $\hat{X}_i(t_l) \neq X_i(t_l)$ and $\hat{X}_i(t_{l+1})$ depends on the packet reception result at time t_{t+1}. If no packet is successfully decoded, then $\hat{X}_i(t_{l+1}) = \hat{X}_i(t_l)$, which happens with probability $(1 - \rho) + \rho PLR_{irsa} = 1 - S_{irsa}m/N_u$. In this case, the distribution of $\Delta_i(t_{l+1})$ is determined by the m-step transition probability of the Markov chain in (25)

$$P(\Delta_i(t_{l+1}) = k \mid \Delta_i(t_l) \neq 0) = q_{irsa}^{(m)}(\Delta_i(t_l), k), \\ k \in \{0, \ldots, m-1, \Delta_i(t_l) + m\}, I_i(t_{l+1}) = 0. \quad (28)$$

On the other hand, if an update packet is successfully decoded, then $\hat{X}_i(t_{l+1}) = X_i(t_l)$. Since the Markov chain describing the remote process is symmetric, without loss of generality, we can assume that $X_i(t_l) = S_1$. Then $\Delta_i(t_{l+1})$ will equal 0, if the remote process remains at state S_1 at time t_{l+1}, i.e., $X_i(t_{l+1}) = S_1$, which happens with probability $p_s^{(m)}(1,1)$, denoting the m-th step transition probability of the Markov chain describing the remote process in (2).

$\Delta_i(t_{l+1})$ will equal $\Delta_i(t_{l+1} - 1) + 1$ if $X_i(t_{l+1}) \neq S_1$. Recall that the random process $\Delta_i(t)$ within a frame is characterized by the Markov chain described by (25). The probability mass function (PMF) for random variable $\Delta_i(t_{l+1} - 1)$ given initial state $\Delta_i(t_l) \neq 0$ can be obtained by

$$P(\Delta_i(t_{l+1} - 1) = k \mid \Delta_i(t_l) \neq 0) = q_{irsa}^{(m-1)}(\Delta_i(t_l), k), \\ k \in \{0, \ldots, m-2, \Delta_i(t_l) + m - 1\}. \quad (29)$$

Therefore, the distribution of $\Delta_i(t_{l+1}) = \Delta_i(t_{l+1} - 1) + 1$ is given by

$$
\begin{aligned}
&P(\Delta_i(t_{l+1}) = k + 1 \mid \Delta_i(t_l) \neq 0) \\
&= q_{irsa}^{(m-1)}(\Delta_i(t_l), k) P(X_i(t_{l+1}) \neq S_1 \mid \Delta_i(t_{l+1} - 1) = k) \\
&= q_{irsa}^{(m-1)}(\Delta_i(t_l), k)(1 - p_t), \\
&k \in \{0, \ldots, m-2, \Delta_i(t_l) + m - 1\}, \ I_i(t_{l+1}) = 1,
\end{aligned}
\tag{30}
$$

where $P(X_i(t_{l+1}) \neq S_1 \mid \Delta_i(t_{l+1} - 1) = k)$ denotes the probability that the source process will not transition to state S_1 at next slot given current AoII $\Delta_i(t_{l+1} - 1) = k$. This probability depends on the value of k. Specifically, if $k = 0$, which implies $X_i(t_{l+1} - 1) = \hat{X}_i(t_{l+1} - 1) = \hat{X}_i(t_l) \neq S_1$, then the probability can be readily obtained as $1 - p_t$. If $k \neq 0$, the situation becomes more complex. Here we approximate this probability as $1 - p_t$ for all k.

To summarize above results, we can write

$$
\begin{aligned}
\alpha_0 &= P(\Delta_i(t_{l+1}) = 0 \mid \Delta_i(t_l) \neq 0) \\
&= (1 - \frac{S_{irsa}m}{N_u}) q_{irsa}^{(m)}(\Delta_i(t_l), 0) + \frac{S_{irsa}m}{N_u} p_s^{(m)}(1, 1), \\
\alpha_k &= P(\Delta_i(t_{l+1}) = k \mid \Delta_i(t_l) \neq 0) \\
&= (1 - \frac{S_{irsa}m}{N_u}) q_{irsa}^{(m)}(\Delta_i(t_l), k) + \frac{S_{irsa}m}{N_u}(1 - p_t) \\
&\quad q_{irsa}^{(m-1)}(\Delta_i(t_l), k - 1), \ k \in \{1, \ldots, m-1\}, \\
\alpha_m &= P(\Delta_i(t_{l+1}) = \Delta_i(t_l) + m \mid \Delta_i(t_l) \neq 0) \\
&= 1 - \alpha_0 - \sum_{k=1}^{m-1} \alpha_k,
\end{aligned}
\tag{31}
$$

and (26) can be expressed as

$$
p_{irsa}(j, k) = \begin{cases}
q_{irsa}^{(m)}(0, k) & j = 0, k = \{0, \ldots, m\} \\
\alpha_k & j \neq 0, k = \{0, \ldots, m-1\} \\
\alpha_m & j \neq 0, k = j + m \\
0 & \text{otherwise.}
\end{cases}
\tag{32}
$$

In the following, we derive expressions for $p_s^{(m)}(1, 1)$ and $q_{irsa}^{(m)}(j, k)$ in (27) and (31) so that we can get a full description of (32).

In general, for a Markov chain, m-step probabilities can be calculated from the m-th power of its one-step transition probability matrix. However, it is difficult to get closed form expressions using this method. In this paper, we consider the case where the average first passage time $\overline{T_t} = 1/p_t \gg m$, which will be explained in the next section. In this situation, some approximations can be made and closed form expressions are obtained. Specifically, there exist many routes that the chain can follow such that it starts from a certain initial state and reaches the destination state after m steps. Some of these routes have probabilities much larger than others, which we call the dominate routes in the rest of the paper. By calculating probabilities of those dominate routes, we can achieve a good approximation.

$p_s^{(m)}(1,1)$ represents the probability that starting from state S_1 the remote process will remain at the same state after m slots. Recall that $\overline{T_t}$ represents the average time needed for the source process to transit back to S_1 after it leaves S_1. Since $\overline{T_t} \gg m$, the remote process will remain at S_1 with very small probability if it leaves state S_1 during the m slots. Therefore, we can approximate $p_s^{(m)}(1,1)$ by considering the dominate route, where the remote process never leaves the initial state:

$$p_s^{(m)}(1,1) = p_R^m. \tag{33}$$

Recall that $q_{irsa}^{(m)}(j,k)$ denotes the probability that starting from $\Delta_i(t) = j$, the AoII will transit to $\Delta_i(t+m) = k$ after m slots. Note that during the m slots, no packets can be decoded and the estimation process keeps the same value. Without loss of generality, we assume that the initial state of the remote process $X_i(t) = S_1$. We need to consider two cases: $\Delta_i(t) = 0$ and $\Delta_i(t) \neq 0$.

In the case of $\Delta_i(t) = 0$, $\hat{X}_i(t) = X_i(t) = S_1$. $\Delta_i(t)$ will be reset to 0 at next slot if the remote process remains at S_1 and increase by 1 otherwise. Since $\overline{T_t} \gg m$, once the remote process leaves S_1, it will be unlikely for the process to return to S_1 at rest slots, which indicates that $\Delta_i(t)$ will increase till the end of the m slots. Therefore, we can approximate $q_{irsa}^{(m)}(0,k)$ by considering the dominate route, where the source process leaves the initial state S_1 after $m - k$ slots for $k \neq 0$ and never leaves the initial state for $k = 0$:

$$q_{irsa}^{(m)}(0,k) = \begin{cases} p_R^m & k = 0 \\ p_R^{m-k}(1 - p_R) & k \in \{1,\ldots,m\}. \end{cases} \tag{34}$$

In the case of $\Delta_i(t) \neq 0$, $\hat{X}_i(t) \neq X_i(t)$. $\Delta_i(t+m)$ will equal $\Delta_i(t)+m$ if the remote process never visits $\hat{X}_i(t)$ during the m slots. This event has probability $(1 - p_t)^m$. Otherwise, $\Delta_i(t+m)$ will take a value in $\{0,\ldots,m-1\}$. First, we consider $\Delta_i(t+m) = 0$. The dominate routes leading to $\Delta_i(t+m) = 0$ are those where the source process first transits to $\hat{X}_i(t)$ at time $t + t_0$, $t_0 \in \{1,\ldots,m\}$ and then remains at $\hat{X}_i(t)$ for the rest of the slots. By adding the probabilities of these routes and observing that $\overline{T_t} = 1/p_t \gg m > 1$ we have

$$q_{irsa}^{(m)}(j,0) = \sum_{t_0=1}^{m} (1 - p_t)^{t_0-1} p_t p_R^{m-t_0}$$

$$= p_t \frac{1 - p_R^m}{1 - p_R} \overset{(3)}{=} \frac{1 - p_R^m}{N_s - 1}, j \neq 0. \tag{35}$$

For $\Delta_i(t+m) = k \in \{1,\ldots,m-1\}$, the dominate routes are those where the remote process first reaches state $\hat{X}_i(t)$ at time $t + m - k$ and leaves the state at the next slot, which happens with probability

$$
\begin{aligned}
q_{irsa}^{(m)}(j,k) &= q_{irsa}^{(m-k)}(j,0)(1 - p_R) \\
&\overset{(35)}{=} \frac{1 - p_R^{m-k}}{N_s - 1}(1 - p_R), \; j \neq 0, \; k \in \{1,\ldots,m-1\}.
\end{aligned}
\tag{36}
$$

Substituting (33), (35) and (36) into (31) we can get

$$
\begin{aligned}
\alpha_0 =& (1 - \frac{S_{irsa}m}{N_u})\frac{1 - p_R^m}{N_s - 1} + \frac{S_{irsa}m}{N_u}p_R^m, \\
\alpha_k =& (1 - \frac{S_{irsa}m}{N_u})\frac{1 - p_R^{m-k}}{N_s - 1}(1 - p_R) + \frac{S_{irsa}m}{N_u}(1 - p_t) \\
& \frac{1 - p_R^{m-k}}{N_s - 1}(1 - p_R) \overset{p_t \ll 1}{\approx} \frac{1 - p_R^{m-k}}{N_s - 1}(1 - p_R), \\
& k \in \{1,\ldots,m-1\}, \\
\alpha_m =& 1 - \alpha_0 - \sum_{k=1}^{m-1}\alpha_k \\
=& 1 - \alpha_0 - p_t\left[m - 1 - (1 - p_R^{m-1})\frac{p_R}{1 - p_R}\right].
\end{aligned}
\tag{37}
$$

Plugging (34) and (37) into (32), we can obtain one-step transition probabilities for the Markov chain describing the evolution of AoII at the first slot of each frame in IRSA, i.e., $p_{irsa}(j, k)$ defined in (26). Leaning on these results, the expression for the average AoII of IRSA is provided as follows.

Proposition 2. *The average AoII of a IRSA system monitoring remote Markov processes of Sect. 2, measured in slots, is given by*

$$
\overline{\Delta}_{irsa} = \overline{\Delta}_{irsa,0} + \overline{\Delta}_{irsa,+},
\tag{38}
$$

where

$$
\overline{\Delta}_{irsa,0} = \theta_0\left\{\frac{m - 1}{2} + \gamma_R/m\left[\gamma_R(1 - p_R^{m-1}) + 1 - m\right]\right\},
$$

$$
\gamma_R = \frac{p_R}{1 - p_R},
$$

$$
\theta_0 = \frac{\alpha_0}{1 + \alpha_0 - p_R^m},
$$

$$
\begin{aligned}
\overline{\Delta}_{irsa,+} =& (1 - \theta_0)\frac{m - 1}{2} + (1 - p_R)\frac{\theta_0 m \alpha_m}{1 - \alpha_m} + \frac{m \alpha_m}{(1 - \alpha_m)^2} \\
& \left[p_R(1 - p_R^{m-1})\frac{N_s\theta_0 - 1}{N_s - 1} + (1 - \theta_0)(m - 1)p_t\right] \\
& + \frac{p_t}{1 - \alpha_m}\left[\gamma_R(m - 1 - \gamma_R + \gamma_R p_R^{m-1})(N_s\theta_0 - 1)\right. \\
& + (1 - \theta_0)m(m - 1)/2\right].
\end{aligned}
$$

Proof. Following similar steps in proofing (17) for SA, it can be shown that the Markov chain characterizing the random process $(\Delta_i(t))_{t \in \Phi}$ is irreducible and aperiodic. Therefore, steady-state probabilities $\{\theta_k\}$, $k \in \mathbb{N}_0$ exist and can be obtained by solving the balance equations:

$$
\begin{cases}
\theta_k = \theta_0 p_R^m + \sum_{j=1}^{\infty} \theta_j \alpha_0 & k = 0 \\
\theta_k = \theta_0 p_{irsa}(0, k) + \sum_{j=1}^{\infty} \theta_j \alpha_k & k \in \{1, \ldots, m-1\} \\
\theta_k = \theta_{\beta_k} (p_{irsa}(\beta_k, \beta_k + m))^{\psi_k} & k \geq m,
\end{cases}
\tag{39}
$$

where $k = \psi_k m + \beta_k$. With the probability normalization equation $\sum_{j=0}^{\infty} \theta_j = 1$, we can write $\theta_0 = \theta_0 p_R^m + (1 - \theta_0)\alpha_0$. Therefore,

$$
\theta_0 = \frac{\alpha_0}{1 + \alpha_0 - p_R^m}.
\tag{40}
$$

Similarly, for $k \in \{1, \ldots, m-1\}$, we can write

$$
\begin{aligned}
\theta_k &= \theta_0 p_{irsa}(0, k) + (1 - \theta_0)\alpha_k \\
&= \theta_0 p_R^{m-k}(1 - p_R) + (1 - \theta_0)\alpha_k
\end{aligned}
\tag{41}
$$

Finally, for $k \geq m$, by referring to (32) and (34) we can obtain

$$
\theta_k = \begin{cases}
\theta_0 (p_R^m)^{\psi_k} & \beta_k = 0 \\
\theta_{\beta_k} (\alpha_m)^{\psi_k} & \beta_k \in \{1, \ldots, m-1\}.
\end{cases}
\tag{42}
$$

It can be concluded that the random process $(\Delta_i(t))_{t \in \Phi}$ is ergodic because it has positive steady-state probabilities.

Segmenting time into frames, the average AoII can be expressed as

$$
\begin{aligned}
\overline{\Delta}_{irsa} &= \lim_{T \to \infty} \frac{1}{T} \sum_{t=1}^{T} \Delta_i(t) \\
&= \lim_{L \to \infty} \frac{1}{L} \sum_{l=1}^{L} \frac{1}{m} \sum_{j=0}^{m-1} \Delta_i(t_l + j) \\
&= \lim_{L \to \infty} \frac{1}{L} \sum_{l=1}^{L} \overline{\Delta}_i^{(l)},
\end{aligned}
\tag{43}
$$

where $\overline{\Delta}_i^{(l)} = \frac{1}{m} \sum_{j=0}^{m-1} \Delta_i(t_l + j)$ represents the average AoII during the l-th frame. Recall that $T_l = \{t_l, \ldots, t_l + m - 1\}$ represents the set of time indexes within the l-th frame and the random process $(\Delta_i(t))_{t \in T_l}$ is Markovian with initial state $\Delta_i(t_l)$ and one-step transition probabilities given in (25).

Next, we derive expressions for the expectation of $\overline{\Delta}_i^{(l)}$ given initial state $\Delta_i(t_l) = k$, which is denoted as $\mathbb{E}\left[\overline{\Delta}_i^{(l)} | \Delta_i(t_l) = k\right]$, by considering two cases: $\Delta_i(t_l) = 0$ and $\Delta_i(t_l) \neq 0$.

For $\Delta_i(t_l) = 0$, with $\overline{T}_t \gg m$, dominate routes for the Markov chain starting from 0 can be identified as that $\Delta_i(t)$ will stay at state 0 for the first j slots and increase in the following slots to $m-1-j$, whose probability can be approximated as $p_R^j(1 - p_R)$. Thus, we have

$$
\begin{aligned}
&\mathbb{E}\left[\overline{\Delta}_i^{(l)} \middle| \Delta_i(t_l) = 0\right] \\
&= \sum_{j=1}^{m-2} p_R^j(1 - p_R)\frac{1}{m}\sum_{k=1}^{m-1-j} k \\
&= \sum_{j=1}^{m-2} p_R^j(1 - p_R)\frac{(j-m)^2 + (j-m)}{2} \\
&= \frac{m-1}{2} + \frac{1}{m}\gamma_R\left[\gamma_R(1 - p_R^{m-1}) + 1 - m\right].
\end{aligned}
\tag{44}
$$

For $\Delta_i(t_l) \neq 0$, with $\overline{T}_t \gg m$, we consider only one dominate route where $\Delta_i(t)$ keeps increasing till the end of the frame. Therefore,

$$
\begin{aligned}
\mathbb{E}\left[\overline{\Delta}_i^{(l)} \middle| \Delta_i(t_l) = k \neq 0\right] &= \frac{1}{m}\sum_{l=0}^{m-1}(k+l) \\
&= k + \frac{m-1}{2}.
\end{aligned}
\tag{45}
$$

Now we can write

$$
\begin{aligned}
\overline{\Delta}_{irsa} &= \lim_{L\to\infty}\frac{1}{L}\sum_{l=1}^{L}\overline{\Delta}_i^{(l)} \\
&\overset{(b)}{=} \sum_{k=0}^{\infty}\theta_k\mathbb{E}\left[\overline{\Delta}_i^{(l)} \middle| \Delta_i(t_l) = k\right] \\
&= \theta_0\mathbb{E}\left[\overline{\Delta}_i^{(l)} \middle| \Delta_i(t_l) = 0\right] + \sum_{k=1}^{\infty}\theta_k\mathbb{E}\left[\overline{\Delta}_i^{(l)} \middle| \Delta_i(t_l) = k\right],
\end{aligned}
\tag{46}
$$

where (b) stems from the ergodicity of the random process $(\Delta_i(t))_{t\in\Phi}$. Substituting (40) and (44) into (46) we get

$$
\overline{\Delta}_{irsa,\,0} = \theta_0\mathbb{E}\left[\overline{\Delta}_i^{(l)} \middle| \Delta_i(t_l) = 0\right].
$$

Plugging (41), (42) and (45) into (46), after some manipulations, we get

$$
\overline{\Delta}_{irsa,\,+} = \sum_{k=1}^{\infty}\theta_k\mathbb{E}\left[\overline{\Delta}_i^{(l)} \middle| \Delta_i(t_l) = k\right],
$$

concluding the proof.   □

4   Numerical Results and Discussion

In this section, we validate the derived analytical expressions via simulations and study the behavior of SA and IRSA in terms of average AoII. In all simulations, we set number of terminals $N_u = 5000$, and degree distribution $\Lambda(x) = x^3$ is employed for IRSA.

The remote Markov process introduced in Sect. 2 is mainly characterized by two parameters: p_t and p_R. Here, we investigate the impact of p_t and p_R from the perspective of $\overline{T_t} = 1/p_t$ and $\overline{T_R} = 1/(1 - p_R)$, which is more conceptually intuitive. Recall that $\overline{T_R}$ represents the mean time duration that the remote process will stay at current state, and $\overline{T_t}$ denotes the mean time needed for the remote process to reach a specific state starting from a different state.

The value of AoII will increase by 1 at each slot if the gateway has an incorrect estimation of the remote process. And it will be reset to 0 whenever the gateway has an correct estimation. This can happen in two circumstances: either the remote process transits to the estimation state at the gateway or an update packet has been successfully decoded at the gateway and the content of the packet brings the correct information of the remote process; one is related to the characteristics of the remote process itself and the other is determined by the RA scheme.

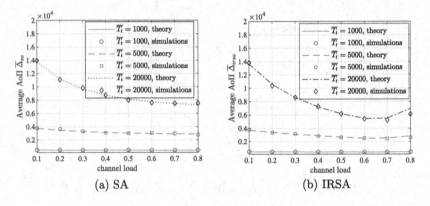

Fig. 2. Average AoII vs. channel load for SA and IRSA; frame size $m = 100$; number of terminals $N_u = 5000$; $\Lambda(x) = x^3$ for IRSA; $\overline{T_R} = 1000$; $\overline{T_t} = 500, 1000,$ and 20000.

4.1   Impact of $\overline{T_t}$

We first study the impact of $\overline{T_t}$ on the average AoII performance for SA and IRSA. The strategy where all terminals keep silent is considered as the baseline scheme for comparison. The average AoII for this scheme can be obtained by setting $S_{sa} = 0$ in (17):

$$\overline{\Delta}_{base} = \frac{1 - p_R}{p_t(p_t + 1 - p_R)}.$$

Figure 2 reports the trends of $\overline{\Delta}_{sa}$ and $\overline{\Delta}_{irsa}$ as a function of the channel load measured in active terminals per slot. It can be observed that both strategies exhibit higher average AoII values with larger $\overline{T}_t$. Indeed, with larger $\overline{T}_t$, it takes longer time for the remote process to transit to the estimation state at the gateway, i.e., to reset AoII to 0, thus leading to higher average AoII.

More interestingly, Fig. 2 indicates that the effect of terminal activity on average AoII highly depends on the value of $\overline{T}_t$. In particular, with $\overline{T}_t = 1000$, both schemes experience approximately the same average AoII at all channel loads. As discussed above, the frequency of resetting AoII to 0 is determined by the Markov source and the packet reception at the gateway. Specifically, the source spends on average $\overline{T}_t$ slots transiting to the estimation state at the gateway while it consumes on average $1/(S_{sa}/N_u)$ and $1/(S_{irsa}/N_u)$ slots to successfully decode an update packet for SA and IRSA respectively. Note that under the collision channel model, since $S_{irsa} < 1$ and $S_{sa} < 1$, we have $1/(S_{sa}/N_u) > N_u$ and $1/(S_{irsa}/N_u) > N_u$. Therefore, when $\overline{T}_t < N_u$, the evolution of AoII will be dominated by the Markov source itself, and the terminal activity will have little effect on the average AoII.

Figure 3 further explores this phenomenon by comparing $\overline{\Delta}_{sa}$ and $\overline{\Delta}_{irsa}$ with $\overline{\Delta}_{base}$ through their ratios, namely $\overline{\Delta}_{sa}/\overline{\Delta}_{base}$ and $\overline{\Delta}_{irsa}/\overline{\Delta}_{base}$. It can be seen that the improvement over $\overline{\Delta}_{base}$ is rather limited for $\overline{T}_t < N_u$, which is of little practical interest. In the following, we mainly focus on the cases where $\overline{T}_t > N_u$. Since we are interested in the mMTC scenario, the number of terminals is much smaller than the number of available resources, i.e., $m \ll N_u$. In this case, we have $m \ll \overline{T}_t$, which has been assumed when deriving the average AoII for IRSA in Sect. 3.

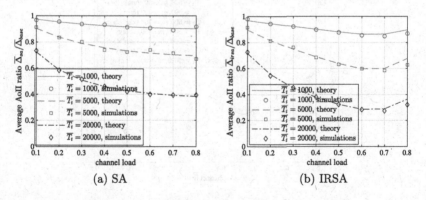

(a) SA   (b) IRSA

Fig. 3. Average AoII ratios $\overline{\Delta}_{sa}/\overline{\Delta}_{base}$ and $\overline{\Delta}_{irsa}/\overline{\Delta}_{base}$ vs. channel load for SA and IRSA; frame size $m = 100$; number of terminals $N_u = 5000$; $\Lambda(x) = x^3$ for IRSA; $\overline{T}_R = 1000$; $\overline{T}_t = 500, 1000,$ and 20000.

4.2 Impact of $\overline{T_R}$ and Frame Size m

A successfully decoded update packet with correct information content will reset current AoII to 0, leading to average AoII reduction. The throughput metric denotes the average number of update packets successfully decoded per slot. Accordingly, a higher throughput with more frequent updating is beneficial for improving the average AoII performance.

On the other hand, the content of the update packet may become incorrect due to the transmission delay, which is 1 for SA and m for IRSA. Although IRSA performs better in terms of throughput compared with SA, it has a longer delay resulted from the frame structure, which may lead to obsolete update packet and overcome the gain brought by throughput. Therefore, for IRSA, there exists an important trade-off between throughput and delay: increasing the frame size m achieves a better throughput performance, but at the same time results in a longer delay. This trade-off obviously depends on $\overline{T_R}$ as $\overline{T_R}$ determines the probability that the update packet will become obsolete with a certain delay.

Figure 4 investigates the role of frame size m in IRSA with two different values of $\overline{T_R}$: 500 and 5000. It can be seen that in the case of a lower $\overline{T_R} = 500$, a larger frame size $m = 300$ penalizes the average AoII at all channel loads in comparison with $m = 50$, indicating that the long delay induced by the larger frame size has overcome the benefits of a higher throughput. While in the case of $\overline{T_R} = 5000$, as the source tends to stay at the current state for a longer time, we observe a preference for a larger frame size at high channel loads (> 0.6).

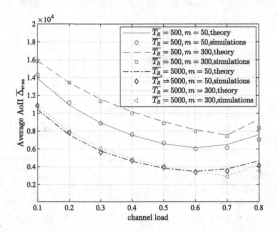

Fig. 4. Average AoII vs. channel load for IRSA; frame size $m = 50, 300$; number of terminals $N_u = 5000$; $\Lambda(x) = x^3$ for IRSA; $\overline{T_R} = 500, 5000$; $\overline{T_t} = 20000$.

This naturally raises the problem of identifying the optimal working point, i.e., the optimal frame size m^* for IRSA given the source parameter T_R and the channel load, which is solved in Fig. 5 based on expression (38) which characterizes the average AoII of IRSA. In general, the optimal frame size increases with the system channel load. At low channel loads with sparse terminal activity, the PLR of IRSA is relatively low. In this situation, increasing the frame size brings limited gains in throughput with a high risk of receiving obsolete information. In contrast, at high loads, the channel becomes more congested, the improvement in throughput with a larger frame size tends to outweigh the risk of receiving an obsolete packet. However, if T_R is small, the risk of an update packet becoming obsolete is relatively high. Then even at high loads, a small frame size is preferred, which is the case for $T_R = 500$ in Fig. 5. In all cases, our derived closed-form expression can be used as an efficient tool to find the optimal frame size for IRSA.

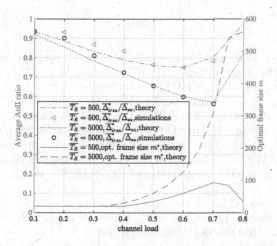

Fig. 5. Optimal frame size m^* for IRSA and Average AoII ratios $\overline{\Delta}^*_{irsa}/\overline{\Delta}_{sa}$ vs. channel load; number of terminals $N_u = 5000$; $\Lambda(x) = x^3$ for IRSA; $\overline{T_R} = 500, 5000$; $\overline{T_t} = 20000$.

We also compare the performance of IRSA adopting optimal frame sizes with SA in Fig. 5, where the average AoII of IRSA is denoted as $\overline{\Delta}^*_{irsa}$ and the comparison is presented in terms of average AoII ratio: $\overline{\Delta}^*_{irsa}/\overline{\Delta}_{sa}$. It can be observed that IRSA outperforms SA at most channel loads. For remote process with large $\overline{T_R}$ IRSA is able to benefit from its advantage of high throughput without risking receiving obsolete packets. However, when $\overline{T_R}$ decreases, IRSA will suffer from the obsolete information and its advantage over SA diminishes. Therefore, for remote process with small $\overline{T_R}$, SA might be an appropriate choice for its simplicity. In this sense, our derived analytical results can be utilized as a convenient tool for choosing the best RA scheme for IoT systems with the knowledge of the characteristics of the Markov remote process to be monitored.

5   Conclusion

In this paper, we investigated RA policies SA and IRSA from the perspective of AoII for IoT systems with Markov sources. Leaning on a Markovian analysis, we tracked the AoII evolution and derived state transition probabilities for SA and IRSA respectively. Closed form expressions of the average AoII were provided for both schemes, which are validated through simulation results. The trade-off between throughput and the risk of receiving packets with incorrect content was explored for IRSA and the key roles played by the frame size m and the Markov source character $\overline{T_R}$ were analyzed and highlighted. The analytical results can be used as an efficient tool for finding the optimal working point for IRSA. Finally, we showed that IRSA can outperform SA significantly under large $\overline{T_R}$. For sources with small $\overline{T_R}$, SA might be a more appropriate choice due to its simplicity.

References

1. i Amat, A.G., Liva, G.: Finite-length analysis of irregular repetition slotted ALOHA in the waterfall region. IEEE Commun. Lett. **22**(5), 886–889 (2018). https://doi.org/10.1109/LCOMM.2018.2812845
2. Atabay, D.C., Uysal, E., Kaya, O.: Improving age of information in random access channels. In: Proceedings of the IEEE INFOCOM Workshops, pp. 912–917 (Jul 2020). https://doi.org/10.1109/INFOCOMWKSHPS50562.2020.9163053
3. Bertsekas, D., Tsitsiklis, J.N.: Introduction to probability. Athena Scientific (2008)
4. Document ETSI EN 301 545–2: Digital Video Broadcasting (DVB); Second Generation DVB Interactive Satellite System (DVB-RCS2); Part 2: Lower Layers for Satellite Standard (2014)
5. Kaul, S.K., Yates, R.D., Gruteser, M.: Real-time status: how often should one update? In: Proceedings of the IEEE INFOCOM, pp. 2731–2735 (Mar 2012). https://doi.org/10.1109/INFCOM.2012.6195689
6. Kriouile, S., Assaad, M.: Minimizing the age of incorrect information for real-time tracking of markov remote sources. In: Proceedings of the IEEE ISIT, pp. 2978–2983 (Jul 2021). https://doi.org/10.1109/ISIT45174.2021.9518209
7. Liva, G.: Graph-based analysis and optimization of contention resolution diversity slotted ALOHA. IEEE Trans. Commun. **59**(2), 477–487 (2011). https://doi.org/10.1109/TCOMM.2010.120710.100054
8. LoRa Alliance Tech. Commitee: LoRaWAN 1.1 Specification (Oct 2017)
9. Maatouk, A., Kriouile, S., Assaad, M., Ephremides, A.: The age of incorrect information: a new performance metric for status updates. IEEE/ACM Trans. Netw. **28**(5), 2215–2228 (2020). https://doi.org/10.1109/TNET.2020.3005549
10. Munari, A.: Modern random access: an age of information perspective on irregular repetition slotted aloha. IEEE Trans. Commun. **69**(6), 3572–3585 (2021). https://doi.org/10.1109/TCOMM.2021.3060429
11. Munari, A., Frolov, A.: Average age of information of irregular repetition slotted ALOHA. In: Proceedings of the IEEE Globecom, pp. 1–6 (Dec 2020)
12. Munari, A., Liva, G.: Information freshness analysis of slotted ALOHA in Gilbert-Elliot channels. IEEE Commun. Lett. **25**(9), 2869–2873 (2021). https://doi.org/10.1109/LCOMM.2021.3092193
13. Ngo, K.H., Durisi, G., i Amat, A.G.: Age of information in prioritized random access. In: Proceedings of the 55th Asilomar Conference on Signals, Systems, and Computers, pp. 1502–1506 (Oct 2021). https://doi.org/10.1109/IEEECONF53345.2021.9723286

14. Paolini, E., Liva, G., Chiani, M.: Coded slotted ALOHA: a graph-based method for uncoordinated multiple access. IEEE Trans. Inf. Theory **61**(12), 6815–6832 (2015). https://doi.org/10.1109/TIT.2015.2492579
15. Saha, S., Sukumaran, V.B., Murthy, C.R.: On the minimum average age of information in IRSA for grant-free mMTC. IEEE J. Sel. Areas Commun. **39**(5), 1441–1455 (2021). https://doi.org/10.1109/JSAC.2021.3065065
16. Sandgren, E., i Amat, A.G., Brännström, F.: On frame asynchronous coded slotted ALOHA: Asymptotic, finite length, and delay analysis. IEEE Trans. Commun. **65**(2), 691–704 (2017). https://doi.org/10.1109/TCOMM.2016.2633468
17. Shao, X., Sun, Z., Yang, M., Gu, S., Guo, Q.: NOMA-based irregular repetition slotted ALOHA for satellite networks. IEEE Commun. Lett. **23**(4), 624–627 (2019). https://doi.org/10.1109/LCOMM.2019.2900319
18. SIGFOX: SIGFOX: the world's leading service provider for Internet of Things (Accessed 14 Sept 2022). www.sigfox.com
19. Wang, Y., Lin, X., Adhikary, A., Grovlen, A., Sui, Y., Blankenship, Y., Bergman, J., Razaghi, H.: A primer on 3GPP narrowband internet of things. IEEE Commun. Mag. **55**(3), 117–123 (2017). https://doi.org/10.1109/MCOM.2017.1600510CM
20. Yates, R.D., Kaul, S.K.: Status updates over unreliable multiaccess channels. In: Proceedings of the IEEE ISIT, pp. 331–335 (Jun 2017). https://doi.org/10.1109/ISIT.2017.8006544
21. Yates, R.D., Kaul, S.K.: Age of information in uncoordinated unslotted updating. In: Proceedings of the IEEE ISIT, pp. 1759–1764 (Jun 2020). https://doi.org/10.1109/ISIT44484.2020.9174098
22. Yavascan, O.T., Uysal, E.: Analysis of slotted ALOHA with an age threshold. IEEE J. Sel. Areas Commun. **39**(5), 1456–1470 (2021). https://doi.org/10.1109/JSAC.2021.3065043

Author Index

J. Zhao (Ed.): WiSATS 2023, LNICST 509, p. 131, 2023.
https://doi.org/10.1007/978-3-031-34851-8

Printed in the United States
by Baker & Taylor Publisher Services